# ALONE

The Badass Psychology of People
Who Like Being Alone

**Bella DePaulo, Ph.D.**

DePaulo, Bella
Alone: The badass psychology of people who like being alone

ISBN-13: 978-1978362277
ISBN-10: 1978362277

FIRST EDITION: October 2017
Printed in the United States of America
10 9 8 7 6 5 4 3 2

Also by BELLA DePAULO

- Singled Out: How Singles Are Stereotyped, Stigmatized, and Ignored, and Still Live Happily Ever After

- How We Live Now: Redesigning Home and Family in the 21st Century

- The Best of Single Life

- Marriage vs. Single Life: How Science and the Media Got It So Wrong

- Singlism: What It Is, Why It Matters, and How to Stop It

- Single Parents and Their Children: The Good News No One Ever Tells You

- Single, No Children: Who Is Your Family?

- The Science of Marriage: What We Know That Just Isn't So

- Single with Attitude: Not Your Typical Take on Health and Happiness, Love and Money, Marriage and Friendship

- Behind the Door of Deceit: Understanding the Biggest Liars in Our Lives

- The Hows and Whys of Lies

- When the Truth Hurts: Lying to Be Kind

- The Lies We Tell and the Clues We Miss: Professional Papers

- Is Anyone Really Good at Detecting Lies? Professional Papers

- Friendsight: What Friends Know that Others Don't

- New Directions in Helping: Volumes 1, 2, and 3

- The Psychology of Dexter

# CONTENTS IN BRIEF

Preface

   I.  The True Meanings of Alone, Loner, and Lonely

  II.  Why People Who Like Being Alone Are Badasses

 III.  The Positive Psychology of Solitude: What's So Great About Being Alone

 IV.  Time Alone: Craving It More Than Ever

  V.  Alone in Public: Dining Alone, Traveling Alone, Alone in a Crowd

 VI.  The Demographic Trend Sweeping the World: Living Alone

VII.  How People Will Try to Scare You About Being Alone – and Why You Should Blow Them Off

VIII.  Keep on Reading: Insights from Great Books on Solitude

# CONTENTS

Preface............................................................................................. 1

I - The True Meanings of Alone, Loner, and Lonely ..................... 3

   1. The Happy Loner..................................................................4

   2. Alone in the World or Alone in Solitude? ............................6

   3. Why Alone is Not the Same as Lonely ................................ 8

   4. What is the Opposite of Loneliness?....................................12

   5. 6 Psychological Insights About Solitude.............................14

   6. 20 Varieties of Solitude .....................................................16

II - Why People Who Like Being Alone Are Badasses................. 19

   7. The Badass Personalities of People Who Like Being Alone ............. 20

   8. Can You Check Off Many of These Signs that You Are Perfectly Happy with Solitude? That Makes You a Badass .....................................25

   9. You Don't Get Coupled Just to Get Through the Holidays: That Makes You a Badass........................................................................ 29

   10. Can You Happily and Unselfconsciously Dine Alone? That Makes You a Badass ..................................................................................32

   11. You Are a Badass Because You Like Being Alone with Your Thoughts and Most Other People Can't Stand It .................................................35

   12. Some People Need to Learn to Be Alone. You, Dear Badass, Are Not One of Them ...................................................................... 38

   13. Those Poor People Who Are Not Badasses: Time Alone Saps Their Willpower ...............................................................................41

III - The Positive Psychology of Solitude: What's So Great About Being Alone.............................................................................. 43

   14. The Psychology of Spending Time Alone...........................44

   15. The Benefits of Solitude ................................................... 48

   16. Another Great Thing About Being Alone...........................51

17. What's So Great About Solitude? People Who Are "Single at Heart" Explain .................................................................... 55

18. The Deep Rewards of a Deeply Single Life ......................... 59

19. Are There Times When You Want to Be Alone, But No One Else Understands? ............................................................... 61

20. Home Alone:  What the Gilmore Girls Got Right ................ 63

21. A Story of Single Life You Haven't Heard Before ............... 65

22. Why Whoopi Goldberg Doesn't Want Anyone to Complete Her ....... 67

**I V - Time Alone: Craving It More Than Ever ..................... 71**

23. The American Psyche: Tipping Toward Solitude? ............... 72

24. What's the #1 Source of Joy in the Lives of 25-to-39-Year-Olds? ..... 76

25. What Does the Richest Person in the World Want? ............. 79

26. What Does the Most Powerful Person in the World Want? ..... 80

27. What Do Many of the Most Influential Philosophers in History Have in Common? ................................................................. 82

28. Why So Many Romantic Partners Want to Be Both Together and Single .................................................................... 86

29. Why Would Committed Couples Live Apart If They Don't Have to? 88

30. Quiet Time: Do We Need It Now More Than Ever? ............. 90

31. A First for Humans? People Now Eat Alone More Often Than with Others ................................................................... 92

32. How Many People Say It Is Important to Have Times When They Are Completely Alone? ................................................ 94

**V - Alone in Public: Dining Alone, Traveling Alone, Alone in a Crowd ....................................................................... 96**

33. More Americans Are Dining Alone and Traveling Alone. Here's Why. ..................................................................... 97

34. The Psychology of Being Alone in Public ......................... 100

35. Has Dining Solo Lost Its Stigma? .................................... 105

36. What's So Great About Traveling on Your Own ................ 108

37. What Do You Really Know About the Experience of Traveling Solo? ................................................................................ 110

38. Alone in a Crowd: There's Something Special About It................... 112

**VI - The Demographic Trend Sweeping the World: .......................
Living Alone .................................................................. 115**

39. Individualism Goes Global: More People Around the World Are Living Alone ..................................................................... 116

40. The Many Different Ways of Living Alone ...................................120

41. Living Alone: 11 Things You Didn't Know ..................................122

42. Best Things About Living Alone ...............................................124

43. Not Monitored, Not Judged: One of the True Joys of Living Alone? ........................................................................................ 127

44. The Least Appreciated Perk of Living Alone ..............................129

45. How Living Alone Will Transform Men ....................................130

**VII - How People Will Try to Scare You About Being Alone – and Why You Should Blow Them Off .......................................132**

46. I've Been Single All My Life. I Rarely Get Lonely. ......................133

47. Is a Solitary Life a Lonely Life? It Could Be Just the Opposite. ........136

48. Are Americans Becoming More and More Isolated? Debunking a Claim that Went Viral ................................................................. 142

49. Isolated People Who Are Not Lonely and Connected People Who Are: A 20-Year Study ...................................................................... 146

50. But What If You *Are* Lonely? ...............................................150

51. Spending Holidays Alone: The Saddest Thing Imaginable or Totally Badass? ................................................................................. 152

52. Aging on Your Own: 5 Things They Never Tell You When They Try to Scare You ............................................................................. 155

53. Will You Grow Old Alone If You Are Single? The Not-Very-Scary Results from 6 Nations................................................................158

54. Is a Solitary Life a Shorter Life? Here's What's Wrong with That Claim ........................................................................................ 162

55. The Ultimate Threat to Single People – You'll Die Alone ................ 165

56. Who Gets Spooked by Stories of Single People Dying Alone? It's Not Who You Think .................................................................... 168

57. The Stunning Appeal of a Story about a Man Who Died Alone ........ 171

58. Brilliant Author and Hospice Worker Makes the Case that Some People Want to Die Alone ..................................................................... 174

**VIII - Keep on Reading: Insights from Great Books on Solitude** 176

59. Insights from the Most Renowned Book on Solitude ........................ 177

60. How to be Alone: 14 Quips and Tips ................................................. 180

61. "Liberty Is a Better Husband" ......................................................... 182

62. Why True Loners Are Awesome – And Why So Many People Thought They Weren't .................................................................................. 185

**About the Author** ................................................................. 188

# Preface

A loneliness panic has swept the nation and the world. For years, the popular press and the annals of academia have been spewing out warnings, in increasingly alarmist tones, that loneliness has reached epic proportions, and that it is killing us.

But amidst all the angst about loneliness, something profoundly important has been overlooked: Some people like being alone. They like their time alone. They like living alone.

In many nations all around the world, the number of people living alone has reached record levels. More and more people are also dining alone, traveling alone, and making their way in public places alone. Studies of married couples in the U.S. show that their lives are less enmeshed than they once were. Some couples are even living apart, in places of their own, not because far-flung jobs or other externalities have forced that upon them, but because they want their own space.

For unknown numbers of people, being alone is not just a preference – it is a craving, a need. Deprived of their time alone for too long, they begin to fantasize about it. Nothing feels quite right until their need for solitude is replenished.

Who are these people who like being alone? Stereotypically, they are the weirdos and the freaks, the scary loners planning shocking acts of violence. New thinking and fresh research upends those caricatures. We now have a better idea of the true personalities of people who like being alone, and they are, well, totally badass.

In June of 2017, I published a post to my "Living Single" blog at *Psychology Today* called "The badass personalities of people who like being alone." Immediately, it took off. It was shared and re-shared. It was republished over and over again, with and without permission. It got picked up nationally and internationally.

That made me realize that there is a real hunger for a different story about the time we spend alone, one that acknowledges that not all people who live alone or spend time alone are lonely or doomed to an early death. Some, in fact, are spectacularly happy and healthy.

I've been writing about people who live single or live alone or like their time alone for decades. In *Alone: The Badass Psychology of People Who Like Being Alone*, I have collected more than 60 of the articles I have published at places such as *Psychology Today, Psych Central*, and the *Washington Post*. Sample what you like or read it cover to cover. Either way, you will come away with a whole new understanding, grounded in research, of what it means to like being alone.

Bella DePaulo
Summerland, CA
October 2017
BellaDePaulo.com

[Note to readers of the print version of this book: Words or phrases that are underlined will show up as links in the e-book version.]

# The True Meanings of Alone, Loner, and Lonely

# The Happy Loner

"Loners" get a bad rap. "Loner" is the label we affix to criminals, outcasts, and just about everyone else we find scary or unsettling. In my all-time favorite book on the topic – _Party of One: The Loners' Manifesto_ – author Anneli Rufus offers a whole different take on the true meaning of "loner." A loner, she says, is "someone who prefers to be alone." That person is so very different than all those who remain on the outside feeling isolated but so desperately wanted to be on the inside, feeling that they belong. The intense but thwarted craving for "acceptance, approval, coolness, companionship" is what sometimes sets off people who go ballistic on their objects of their desires.

In an essay in the _Guardian_, Barbara Ellen lets us know that she has also had enough of the fear and the pity for people who actually _like_ their time alone. Here's how she opens her commentary:

There used to be a fashion for scaremongering surveys about single women, saying things like: "Eight out of 10 women are going to die alone, surrounded by 17 cats." But to that I would mentally add: "Or it could all go horribly wrong." To my mind, aloneness never necessarily equated with loneliness. It wasn't a negative, something to be avoided, feared or endured.

In the tradition of Anneli Rufus (and everyone else who recognizes that alone and lonely are not the same thing), Ellen know that the kind of solitude that is chosen is a whole different experience than the type that is unwelcome. Riffing on a headline proclaiming that "Britain is the loneliness capital of Europe," Ellen offers an alternative perspective:

This study could just as well be interpreted as saying that many Britons are self-reliant problem-solvers, respectful of other people's privacy – and what's wrong with that? Isn't this the modern British definition of neighbourliness: not over-chummy and intrusive, but friendly, considerate and, most importantly, happy to sign for your Amazon parcels?

Barbara Ellen also poses a question that we should all ponder: Why is it that sociability is considered a skill, whereas the ability to be alone is seen as weird? As she notes:

Personally, I'd be more likely to distrust people who can't bear time with themselves. What's wrong with *them* that they can't abide their own company – what are they trying to hide in the crowd?

# Alone in the World or Alone in Solitude?

For such a little word, "alone" carries some big meanings. Sometimes "alone" is used to mean "single," and I have often found that troubling. When other people are discussing a single person and they say, "she's alone," they often do so with sadness and pity. What they mean is, "She doesn't have anyone" or "He's alone in the world."

There are single people who truly are alone in the world, just as there are married people who fit that description. (Having a spouse is no guarantee of having someone who cares about you or even talks to you.) On the average, though, single people are more connected to other people than married people are. I've written often about how single people have more friends, do more to maintain their ties with siblings and parents and friends and neighbors, do more to participate in the life of their cities and towns, and do more than their share of caring for aging parents and others who need help. In contrast, when couples move in together or get married, they tend to become more insular. That happens even if they don't have children.

Single people who fit this typical pattern of maintaining a diversity of personal relationships are probably less vulnerable than, say, married people who invest all their relationship capital in their spouse. Research on susceptibility to depression is consistent with that suggestion. So is research on "emotionships," which are the relationships we have with other people that are emotion-specific (for example, looking to different people when we are angry vs. happy vs. sad).

"Alone in the world" is the ominous meaning of "alone." There is another, more uplifting meaning, that many people embrace – single people in particular, and especially those who are single at heart. "Alone" can mean alone in solitude – having time and space to yourself. To the many people who savor their solitude, time alone is a blessing and a gift. To some (myself included), it may even feel like a necessity. To those who crave solitude rather than fearing it, time alone can offer wonderful opportunities for creativity, relaxation, rejuvenation, reflection, and spirituality.

When I spent some time asking people about their ideal living situations, I found that everyone wants some time alone and some time with other people, but the proportions vary enormously from person to person. When seeking time to themselves, people are making room in their lives for that positive, nourishing, and uplifting sense of being alone. When seeking meaningful connections with other people, they are trying to keep that other sense of aloneness, being alone in the world, at bay. When we find just the right balance of time alone and time with others, it is magical.

# Why Alone is Not the Same as Lonely

With more and more people living single and living alone, and so much hand-wringing about loneliness, it has never been more important to understand the difference between the kind of aloneness that people seek out and savor (*not* loneliness) and the kind of aloneness that hurts (loneliness). That's what I talked about when Peace Talks Radio asked me to participate in their special show, "Considering Loneliness." Here's the transcript of my part of the show.

Peace Talks Radio Host Paul Ingles talks with Dr. Bella DePaulo, Project Scientist, University of California at Santa Barbara, author of "Singled Out: How Singles are Stereotyped, Stigmatized, and Ignored, and Still Live Happily Ever After and How We Live Now: Redefining Home and Family in the 21st Century."

**Paul Ingles:** Dr. Bella DePaulo is an author and visiting professor at the University of California at Santa Barbara. Dr. DePaulo, you've also authored a blog called "The Happy Loner" that begins: "Loners get a bad rap. Loner is the label we affix to criminals, outcasts and just about everyone else we find scary or unsettling."

Then you quote author Anneli Rufus who wrote a different take that a loner is quote "someone who prefers to be alone" which you say is different from those who remain on the outside feeling isolated but desperately want to be on the inside. Help me understand the distinction. It sounds to me like you accept the more troubling definition of loner, but just want to make room for Loner 2.0 or Loner B who just prefers to be alone. Is that fair?

**Bella DePaulo:** Yes. Well, Anneli Rufus says that a loner is someone who prefers to be alone, so that's her central basic definition and she thinks that when we call these serial killers "loners" and we affix that kind of dark, menacing meaning to loner, we're distorting the true meaning of loner.

But let me say that whether being alone, living alone is a good or bad thing depends on how you got there. So if you got there because you want it and you love it and you crave it, that's great. If you got there because, let's say a spouse died, that's more difficult although some people find that once a spouse dies, they come into their own in their own space and time.

The real problematic person living alone is the one who has been rejected, who has been ostracized, particularly if they've been chronically ostracized. I think that can be an ingredient to real deep anger and the potential for violence.

**Ingles:** So let's say your "Loner B" in our little construct here, you prefer to be alone. Is it valuable to be even concerned about the claims of researchers that they might be at risk of becoming "Loner A" like distrustful of society or prone to feeling rejected? Is it valuable, if you choose to be alone, to be aware of your place on the continuum and have an awareness of this conversation?

**DePaulo:** I suppose so, but you know what's really interesting? There's a whole cottage industry of loneliness. If you went on Google and typed "loneliness," you'd probably get tens of thousands of returns and yet the kind of research that would look at whether people have chosen to be alone or not is strikingly missing. So we really don't know if the people who choose to be alone, who savor their solitude, who get great creative work done, get great restorative benefits, we don't know if they are prone to some of the same negative risks that we've heard about so often in the general literature on loneliness. We just don't know. That's my scientific answer.

**Ingles:** Okay and do you have another answer?

**DePaulo:** Yes, I wonder about it. Imagine if we tried to force everyone to live with other people because we think that would somehow cure loneliness. Would it really? I think especially about the change over time and how older people live. It used to be that older people, say if a spouse died, they would almost automatically end up living with other people, often their grown children. Now that older people have Social Security and other ways of actually buying their own independence, more and more of them are choosing to live alone and they're certainly choosing to stay outside of institutions if they can possibly afford it and so it seems like people are making a choice and so I think we should be cautious about demonizing people who live alone or thinking: you poor thing. Your life is going to be nasty, brutish and short because they've chosen this. Many people who live alone could find other people to live with, but that's not what they want to do.

**Ingles:** *Well let's see, let me go here with this then; one of your books is entitled Singled Out: How Singles Are Stereotyped, Stigmatized and Ignored and Still Live Happily Ever After, so let me look at the first half of that title to start because it sounds like it's kind of what we were talking about here. It sounds like that you're citing a societal preference for coupling.*

**DePaulo:** Yes, absolutely.

**Ingles:** Are you suggesting that by stereotyping, stigmatizing and ignoring signals that society could be amplifying feelings of loneliness?

**DePaulo:** Yes, it is, and ironically, what it could also be doing is pushing people to marry who really don't feel like it's right for them and what happens then is you have people who end up lonelier than they would have been because they're marrying because they think they should marry, because they think it's the only legitimate, respected, celebrated option and so then they end up with what is probably the most painful kind of loneliness; the loneliness you experience when there is someone lying there right beside you.

**Ingles:** What would you call on society to do for its part in quelling loneliness brought on in part by those attitudes about singles? I mean if someone listening says, "Oh yeah, I guess I have thought that about singles," what would you suggest they change in their behavior or their attitude that might tone it down a little bit?

**DePaulo:** I think they should realize that there are <u>so many ways to live</u> in contemporary American society. That's one of the joys of living in this time and place.

# What is the Opposite of Loneliness?

On the eve of her graduation from Yale, Marina Keegan wrote an essay that, within about a week, would be read by well over a million people from 98 nations. It was called "The Opposite of Loneliness."

But what is the opposite of loneliness? Keegan opened her essay by noting that we don't have a word for it, but whatever it is, she found it at Yale:

> "It is not quite love and it's not quite community; it's just this feeling that there are people, an abundance of people, who are in this together. Who are on your team. When the check is paid and you stay at the table. When it's four A.M. and no one goes to bed…

> "Yale is full of tiny circles we pull around ourselves. A cappella groups, sports teams, houses, societies, clubs. These tiny groups that make us feel loved and safe and part of something even on our loneliest nights…"

That essay now opens a collection of Keegan's writings published under the same title, "The Opposite of Loneliness." The question it poses, what is the opposite of loneliness, still resonates.

For people who are "single at heart," I think the opposite of loneliness is single life.

People who are single at heart live their best, most meaningful, and most authentic lives as single people. I'm one of them. I rarely feel lonely, and when I do, it is usually when I'm with other people. One time, when I was living in Charlottesville, I was walking the downtown mall with a friend I always loved talking to – she's smart, wryly funny, and great at getting to matters of depth. We happened upon a big table of colleagues who were laughing and talking. She wanted to join them. I sat for a while, but their conversation was so superficial and so inane, it made me feel lonely. I made an excuse and left.

Another time, two couples wanted to treat me for my birthday. I looked forward to it. But they spent the night talking about babies and daycare. The whole night. That, rather spending my birthday home alone, is the definition of loneliness.

I like the examples Keegan gives of the opposite of loneliness. But I'd add to them the experiences of being all by yourself, and feeling so engaged in whatever you are doing that you don't even notice how much time has passed or that you're actually pretty tired. (I think it is an example of what Mihaly Csikszentmihalyi calls "flow.") The opposite of loneliness is realizing the answer to what you were puzzling over when you weren't trying to figure it out — during a long walk, for instance, or in the shower or just as you are falling asleep or waking up. The opposite of loneliness is feeling grateful for all the people in your life you cherish, even (especially?) when you don't see them all the time.

The opposite of loneliness is JOMO — the Joy of Missing Out. For me, that's when I'm so delighted not to feel obligated to participate in social events that don't interest me. I stay home and revel in my solitude, or pursue the social engagements that really do engage me.

Alone is not lonely. Alone is a neutral description of a state that can be experienced any number of ways. Loneliness is, by definition, painful. The opposite of loneliness is contentment or joy. It is living your most meaningful life, the life you want to live rather than the life you think you should be living. For me, the opposite of loneliness is living single.

# 6 Psychological Insights About Solitude

People who are single-at-heart love the time they have to themselves. In fact, when thinking about spending time alone, just about all of them react with something like, "Ah, sweet solitude," and almost none of them react with, "Oh, no, I might be lonely!"

With more and more people living single, and more and more people living alone, a better understanding of solitude is becoming increasingly important. In 2014, *The Handbook of Solitude* was published. One of my favorite chapters in the book is "Experiences of Solitude," by James Averill and Louise Sundararajan. It is a chapter that acknowledges the potential negative experiences of solitude, such as loneliness and boredom, but has far more to say about what can make solitude so sweet. Here are six of the authors' insights.

**#1** There is a difference between *authentic solitude*, in which the experience of being alone is mostly positive, and *pseudo-solitude*, which feels mostly like loneliness. Do you know what it is?

It's *choice*: "...authentic solitude is typically based on a decision to be alone; in contrast, pseudo-solitude, in which loneliness predominates, involves a sense of abandonment or unwanted isolation."

**#2** Loneliness is not all negative. It can actually be part of an authentic solitude experience, as, for example, when people drift in and out of different feelings, including feelings of loneliness, when they are alone. Loneliness can also be motivating, as when it pushes people to figure out solutions to their problems. Only when loneliness dominates the experience of being alone and seems insurmountable does the experience get classified as pseudo-solitude.

**#3** Do we appreciate solitude more as we grow older? I don't know of any definitive data on this, but the authors believe that we do, as did Einstein when he said, "I live in that solitude which is painful in youth, but delicious in years of maturity." Averill and Sundararajan believe that "the sentiment is true of many people of advanced age, who have learned to find solitude delicious but who are reluctant to admit the fact due to cultural prejudices."

**#4** How can we understand how some people come to be good at being alone and others just can't handle it? Again, I don't know any great data on that, but the authors point to the 20th century psychoanalyst, Donald Winnocott, who believed that experiences during infancy are important. As the authors explained, "he posited that only those people who as infants were free to explore and independently occupy themselves in the security of their mothers' presence will as adults have the capacity to be alone."

**#5** It is possible to experience solitude vicariously – for example, through art or poetry. Certain portrayals of nature can be especially effective.

**#6** The kinds of opportunities we now have to experience solitude were largely missing in the past. "For example, in colonial America, young people were expected to establish a household as soon as they had the means to live independently. Within a household privacy was rarely possible, even in bed; and since households served multiple functions (educational, commercial, etc.), they were, in turn, under constant guidance and surveillance by the community."

# 6

# 20 Varieties of Solitude

In "Experiences of solitude," a chapter in _The Handbook of Solitude_, James Averill and Louise Sundararajan described twenty different experiences of solitude. Statistical analyses showed that the experiences clustered into five groups, with a few of the experiences not fitting clearly into just one of the groups. (Those are listed under "other experiences of solitude.")

In research by Yao Wang reviewed in the chapter, American and Chinese university students rated the desirability of the 20 different experiences of time alone. Using the American ratings, I have listed the five main groups in the order of desirability. So, for Americans, experiences of freedom were the most desirable experiences of being alone. Within each of the five groups, I also arranged the specific examples the same way – the ones rated most desirable by the Americans are listed first.

The American and Chinese ratings were most different for _freedom_ and _problem-solving_. Americans found the experience of freedom especially more desirable than the Chinese did (though the Chinese rated it on the desirable end of the scale) and the Chinese rated the opportunity for problem-solving as more desirable than the Americans did.

## 1. Freedom

- _**Inner peace**_: "You feel calm and free from the pressures of everyday life."

- _**Freedom**_: "You feel free to do as you wish, without concern for social rules."

- _**Daydreaming**_: "You engage in fantasies where you could do anything you desire."

## 2. Enlightenment

- ***Self-discovery***: "You gain insight into your fundamental values and goals, unique strengths, and weaknesses."

- ***Enlightenment***: "You gain better realization of life's meaning and significance."

- ***Emotional refinement***: "Being alone provides an opportunity to cultivate and refine your emotions."

- ***Self-enrichment***: "You use the time to enrich yourself and to broaden your perspective."

- ***Creativity***: "Being alone stimulates novel ideas or innovative ways of expressing yourself."

- ***Problem-solving***: "You think about specific problems and plan a course of action."

## 3. Intimacy

- ***Reminiscence***: "You recall events you have experienced or people you have known."

- ***Intimacy***: "You feel especially close to someone you care about."

## 4. Relaxation

- ***Relaxation***: "You use the time to rest or sleep and to recharge."

- ***Recreation***: "You engage in distracting activities, for example, watch television and surf the web."

## 5. Loneliness

- ***Alienation***: "You feel isolated from the rest of society, left out, and forgotten."

- ***Boredom***: "You wish for something to occupy your mind."

- **Loneliness**: "You feel unappreciated, depressed, anxious, and lonely."

## Other Experiences of Solitude

- **Harmony**: "Everything seems interconnected with everything else; you are in balance with the world."

- **Self-transcendence**: "As in meditation, you have a sense of transcending everyday distinctions and concerns."

- **Heightened sensory awareness**: "Sights and sounds seem magnified; you observe small things that you ordinarily wouldn't notice."

- **Longing**: "Yearning for people or things beyond your reach at the moment."

# Why People Who Like Being
# Alone Are Badasses

# The Badass Personalities of People Who Like Being Alone

There are people who like being alone, maybe even love it. What do you think they are like?

Does your mind leap immediately to the misanthrope or to the dreaded loner hiding away somewhere plotting the next mass murder? As Anneli Rufus told us in her wonderful *Party of One: The Loners' Manifesto*, those stereotypes don't capture real loners. True loners are people who embrace their alone time. Others, such as those who lash out, are typically alone against their will. They want to be included. They want to be loved by the objects of their desire. But they've been excluded and rejected instead. That exclusion and rejection (among other things) is what fuels their hostility and rage.

What's the truth about people who like being alone? What are they really like? Thanks to some newly developed scales for measuring attitudes toward being alone, we now have research-based answers.

First, though, we need to understand what it means to like being alone. One sense of "alone" refers to spending time alone. The "Desire for Being Alone" scale, developed by Birk Hagemeyer and his colleagues, measures that.

People who score high on the **desire to be alone** AGREE with items such as:

> *When I am alone, I feel relaxed.*

> *I like to be completely alone.*

They DISAGREE with items such as:

> *I feel uncomfortable when I am alone.*

> *Being alone quickly gets to be too much for me.*

A second meaning of alone is the way it is used to refer to people who are single. (I think that usage is misleading and inappropriate, but I'll save that argument for another day.) Thinking about single life as something some people fear, Stephanie Spielmann and her colleagues developed a "Fear of Being Single" scale. I'm interested in the personality characteristics of people who are UNAFRAID of being single, so I just reversed their scale.

People who are **UNAFRAID of being single** DISAGREE with items such as:

> *I feel anxious when I think about being single forever.*
>
> *If I end up alone in life, I will probably feel like there is something wrong with me.*

## Details of the Studies

*Participants*

Personality was measured for two groups of people in the "Fear of Being Single" studies. One group consisted of 301 people recruited online, with an average age of 29. Only 33 were married; 131 were single and not dating, and the others were dating. The other group was comprised of 147 Canadian undergraduates, average age of 19. Only 2 were married, 105 were single and not dating, and the others were dating. Results were averaged across both groups.

Two groups of German adults participated in the "Desire for Being Alone" studies, and unfortunately for people like me who are interested in single people, all the participants were coupled – they had been in a serious sexual relationship for at least a year. The first study included 476 participants (average age, 35), and the results were averaged across the men and the women. The second study included 578 heterosexual couples (average age, 42). Results were reported separately for the men and the women.

## Personality Characteristics

The "Big Five" personality characteristics were measured for all the participants in both sets of studies:

*Neurotic*: tense, moody, worries a lot

*Open*: original, curious, imaginative

*Extraverted*: Outgoing and sociable, talkative, assertive

*Agreeable*: considerate and kind, trusting, cooperative

*Conscientious*: reliable, organized, thorough

The studies of people who like spending time alone also included a measure of their *sociability*, as measured by items such as, "I find people more stimulating than everything else."

The studies of people unafraid to be single included measures of six more characteristics:

*Relationship-contingent self-esteem*: the extent to which a person's self-esteem is contingent on how their romantic relationship is going (when they have one)

*Need to belong*: People who are high in the "need to belong" are especially likely to agree with statements such as "I need to feel that there are people I can turn to in times of need."

*Hurt feelings proneness*: These are people whose feelings are easily hurt.

*Rejection sensitivity*: People who are particularly sensitive to rejection are especially likely to expect to be rejected and feel anxious about it.

*Loneliness*: Measured by items such as, "How often do you feel that you lack companionship?"

*Depression*: Measured by items such as, "I felt that I could not shake off the blues even with help from my family or friends."

## The Findings: What People Who Like Being Alone Are Really Like

If our stereotypes about people who like being alone were true, then we would find that they are neurotic and closed-minded. In fact, just the opposite is true.

People who like spending time alone, and people who are unafraid of being single, are especially **unlikely to be neurotic**. They are NOT the tense, moody, worrying types.

People who like spending time alone, and people who are unafraid of being single, are also more likely than others to be ***open-minded***. They are original, curious, and imaginative.

People who are unafraid of being single are more agreeable (considerate, kind, trusting) than people who are afraid of being single. (People who like spending time alone are no more or less agreeable than people who don't.)

People who are unafraid of being single are also more conscientious than those who are afraid. (Results were not consistent for people who like spending time alone.)

The question I am asked most often about the personality of people who are single is whether they are more introverted. The one relevant study suggests that they probably are. But research on single people typically includes all single people, whether they want to be single or not. The studies I'm describing here tell us about people who are unafraid of being single (or about people who like spending time alone).

People who are unafraid of being single were more extraverted than those who are afraid of being single. Perhaps this finding is consistent with the research showing that single people, on the average, have more friends than married people do, and do more to maintain their relationships with their friends, neighbors, siblings, and parents. But again, the research on the social ties of single people includes all single people, not just those who are unafraid of being single.

The people who like spending time alone were not any more or less extraverted than the people who do not like spending time alone, but they did score as less sociable. Those two scales (extraversion, sociability) measure similar things so it is odd that they did not produce consistent findings.

All the other personality characteristics were measured only in the studies of people who are unafraid of being single. The results were resoundingly affirming. People who are unafraid of being alone are ***not overly sensitive to rejection*** and they ***don't get their feelings hurt too easily***. When they are in romantic relationships, their own ***self-esteem does not depend on how those relationships are faring***. They ***do not have a particularly strong need to belong***. They are ***less likely to be lonely*** and ***less likely to be depressed***.

Put all that together with their openness, agreeableness, conscientiousness, extraversion, and low levels of neuroticism, and people who are unafraid of being single look totally badass.

The people who are unafraid of being single are not just talking a good game. Other studies looked at their behaviors and those results were affirming, too. People who are unafraid of being single have standards. For example, in speed dating events, they give out their contact information to fewer people. And, when they do get into a romantic relationship and find it unsatisfying, they are more likely to break it off than are people who are afraid of being single.

Despite all that is good and affirming about people who are unafraid of being single, they cannot expect to be celebrated or even respected by other people. People who like being single, who choose to be single, are threatening cherished worldviews about what people should want and how they should feel. Other people evaluate them more harshly than single people who wish they were coupled – even expressing more anger toward them.

As more and more people openly embrace their single lives, maybe things will change. Happy singles will become part of our cultural landscape, and people who are threatened by them will recede to the fringes.

# Can You Check Off Many of These Signs that You Are Perfectly Happy with Solitude? That Makes You a Badass

If you are someone who likes having time to yourself and space to yourself, and just never felt in tune with all the relentless matrimania (the over-the-top hyping of marriage and weddings and coupling), there have always been other people like you. But now, more than ever before, those people are speaking out and getting heard. What's more, what they have to say sometimes, in an instant, becomes wildly popular.

An example is an article first posted by John Warwick at Elite Daily in March of 2015, "Alone isn't lonely: 10 signs you're perfectly happy with solitude." It has been shared more than 69,000 times. More than 2,300,000 people have Liked it.

I, too, appreciate Warwick's 10 signs. I relate to many of them and I like how some of them dovetail with what I've learned about people who are single at heart. So, I'll share them first. But then I will share my reservations, not with the signs but with Warwick's framing of what this says about the people who read the 10 signs and realize that yes, I am someone who is perfectly happy with solitude.

Here are the 10 signs that you are perfectly happy with solitude. (For Warwick's discussion of each, take a look at the original article.)

1. You love free weekends.

2. You'll go to the movies on your own.

3. You're comfortable with eating out by yourself.

4. You prefer drinking on your own.

5. You travel the world solo.

6. You hate sharing beds.

7. You find driving alone calming.

8. You neglect your phone, a lot.

9. You can be socially MIA for long periods of time.

10. You see "clingy" as an unattractive trait.

A good example of the single-at-heart sensibility of some of these signs is what Warwick says about traveling alone: "The idea of discovering the world on your own doesn't scare you – it exhilarates you." <u>Stereotypes of single people</u> insist that they are alone and lonely, cowering in their apartments, too fearful to face the world. In real life, many singles fit Warwick's description: they are exhilarated even by experiences that other people find intimidating.

Warwick's discussion of #10 also resonates with the single-at-heart in important ways. For example, he notes: "You need that space to be alone, physically and mentally." The "need" word is important here. People who vastly prefer living with other people and being with people a great deal of the time just don't get it about how wanting to be alone can feel more like a need than a mere preference. But it can.

Also in the discussion of #10 is this: "Your decisions are wholeheartedly your decisions, and you love that." There is research to support the significance of this preference for handling things on your own. In my preliminary research on people who are <u>single at heart</u>, I've found that they differ from people who are not single-at-heart by their desire to make their own decisions. And in a study of people who were 40 or older and had been <u>single all their lives</u>, the trait of self-sufficiency served them in a way that it did not serve comparable people who were married. For the always-single, the more self-sufficient they were, the less likely they were to experience negative emotions. For the married people, the more self-sufficient their personalities, the more likely they were to experience negative feelings.

Now for my reservations. Speaking of people who are perfectly happy with solitude, Warwick says that "there are a select few who don't feel relationships are their top priority." In fact, though, we have no idea how many people feel this way. No one has ever done the relevant research. And even if researchers were to approach a big, nationally representative sample of adults and ask them about such things, there would still be a huge impediment. Because craving time on your own is so rarely acknowledged or appreciated in our cultural conversations, because matrimania is rampant, and because wanting to be in romantic relationships is portrayed as normal and maybe even inevitable, it is difficult for people who love their solitude to own that. Too many of them are wondering whether they don't really like their time alone, they just haven't met the right person. Or maybe they have internalized the cultural narrative that if they are not goo-goo over romance and coupling, there's something wrong with them. So I'm not sure how many people who really do love their solitude more than they love romantic relationships would say so to a researcher – or even to themselves.

My biggest objection, though, is with something else Warwick says about people who are perfectly happy with solitude: "Their focus is satisfying their needs, and their needs only." But think about people who really need to be with other people. When they spend time with other people, *they are satisfying their own need to do so*. Are they fulfilling someone else's similar need in the process? Most likely. But I don't think that counts as something for which they deserve extra credit. If the other person isn't fulfilling their needs, they will probably flee. (Unless they stay because they are scared of being alone.) And I think that means that what they are doing really is about their needs, and their needs only.

So who is more attentive to the needs of others: People who put romantic relationships at the center of their lives or those who are more inclined toward solitude? If we take the difference between married and single people as one (imperfect) way of assessing that, then we already know the answer. There are <u>many relevant studies</u>. Single people are more likely than married people to support, stay in touch with, and exchange help with their parents, siblings, neighbors, and friends. They are also more often the ones to provide the long-term intensive care that other people need when they are sick or disabled or elderly. Follow the same people over time as they go from being single to getting married, and you will see the development of insularity. The same people who were caring and connected as single people become focused mostly on their spouse (and children, if they have any) once they marry.

So, don't tell me it is the solitude lovers who are focused solely on their own needs.

# You Don't Get Coupled Just to Get Through the Holidays: That Makes You a Badass

I know that I'm supposed to feel self-conscious around the holidays, walking into all those holiday parties on my own when so many others are coupled-up. But I don't. In fact, I feel both happy and proud. Happy, because I'm a sociable person and I like some of these gatherings; and happy because I also love my solitude, and after the party is over, I can go home to some.

The proud part is more interesting: I like it that I don't grab onto someone just to try to fit in at a time of such relentless coupling.

There are people who do practice that anxiety-grab, and some of them hold on tight all the way through to Valentine's Day. Yahoo found, when they surveyed users of their Personals page, that Valentine's Day is part of "National Break-Up Season" -- a time when "people tend to 'put up' with current relationships in order to have a partner for holiday gatherings." Around then, coupled people are twice as likely to be thinking of breaking up, and once that last chocolate-covered cherry is gone, so too is their sweetheart.

A scientific approach to the same question also showed that couples are especially likely to break up during Valentine's season. Unsurprisingly, the people in relationships that were not so great were especially likely to break up. But even the people in the best relationships did not feel any better about their partners during Valentine's season than any other time of year.

So here's a little party game you can play, on your own or with any number of others. Look around you at all the different parties, through December and New Year's and Valentine's Day. See if you can spot the couples who are just faking it. Some will be rent-a-couples - they are just hanging out together as temps. Others, though, will be truly, officially, legally married.

I remember once going to an evening social event connected to a scientific conference. One very famous social psychologist arrived late to the gathering (his wife was already there) and engaged in a very public display of affection. Now I don't mean your garden-variety PDA; I mean the kind that might even make an enlightened high school student blush. I immediately thought to myself: They are doomed.

They were.

Now I'm not anti-coupling. Really, I'm not. Maybe because I love being single, I can observe couples who seem to be a great match and enjoy that, too. My favorite example comes from my own parents. They and my sibs and their kids and partners used to get together occasionally for a week at Duck beach in North Carolina. My mother, especially, seemed to love these gatherings since by then, all four of us grown "kids" were spread far and wide across the country. One night after dinner, when everyone was just relaxing and talking, my father said he was going out to put gas in the car. And my mother said she would go with him. To think that, even with all her kids and grandkids around, she would want to go out to do errands with her husband - well, that seemed sort of bewildering and also kind of sweet. (Are you thinking up snarky ways to smash my reveries, like suggesting that maybe she wasn't so enamored of all of us as I'd like to think, or that perhaps "put gas in the car" was code for something that even grown kids try not to picture their parents doing? Well, save them! No, really, go ahead and post them.)

I said I'm not against marriage or coupling. But I am against compulsory coupling. I'm <u>against the stigmatizing of those who are not coupled</u>, whether by choice or by happenstance. One way to stop the stigma is to stop playing along with the game. If there is not someone you really want to be with over the holidays, then go to all those parties on your own. (Of course, I think party invitations should include friends, but that's a different topic.) Even if you do wish you were coupled and it is hard to walk in uncoupled, do it and feel proud. Embrace and enjoy your inner smug singlehood.

Don't do it just for yourself. Every time you show up as your own complete person, rather than appearing in your couple costume, you make it easier for everyone else who is also single for the holidays or for good (and I do mean good). And though they probably won't admit it, you are probably also helping the people who just can't wait for the holiday season to end, so they can return their rental partner. Maybe next year they'll show up on their own.

# 10

# Can You Happily and Unselfconsciously Dine Alone? That Makes You a Badass

The first time I ever taught a course on singles (called "Singles in society and in science"), I suggested that the students go out to lunch or dinner alone. They were really into the course and they upped the ante – they insisted it must be dinner, not lunch. Some went further – they went to a really nice restaurant. Another decided that all props were off limits – he thought it would be cheating to be able to read, for example.

Since the assignment was my idea, I thought I should do it too. So during the same time period when all of the students were headed out to dinner on their own, I went there too.

We had a great time exchanging stories afterwards. That was many years ago (in Charlottesville, Virginia, in the late 90s) but I now realize that one of the main themes of our experiences was that the people who were most uncomfortable were *not* those of us who were dining in a nice restaurant on our own. It was everyone else.

The uneasiness started with just telling other people what we planned to do. One student described her roommate's reaction: "You have got to be kidding!" Then there was the matter of trying to get seated. One person was totally ignored by the hostess, who just assumed she was waiting for someone else to show up and join her. Another was led into a separate room with no other diners – until she objected.

Now I have to confess that I did feel a bit uncomfortable, but I think it was because I was the only real diner in the entire restaurant! I chose a new place to try out for the experience, an upscale spot, but I guess it hadn't caught on. Other than serving me, the restaurant personnel spent the evening serving one another.

I have been thinking about this because *Cosmopolitan* magazine featured a story by Jen Doll, "Just one? A girl's guide to going solo." The reporter opened by admitting that even though she considers herself "an independent, relatively self-assured, fully grown-up" person, when she goes to restaurants, movies, bars, or the gym, she always has company. So she set out to try each of those activities, and more, on her own.

For me, a highlight of her restaurant experience was that when she walked into her neighborhood restaurant, she found that most of the other diners were...other people dining solo! I wish someone had been keeping track of restaurant diners over the years. I wonder whether, with the increase in the number of single people and the rise in people living alone and perhaps a lessening of self-consciousness in an era saturated with social media, the prospect of sitting in restaurants on your own is just not as daunting as it once was.

The reporter was not as eager to head out on her own as my students had been all those years ago. Like my students (and me), she learned something in the process. Here's how she describes one of her experiences going to a bar by herself:

> "Then into the bar came a woman who sat herself down next to me and opened a book and ordered dinner, all in one smooth move. She was by herself, but entirely unperturbed about that. She was the dining-alone person I wanted to be, effortlessly sipping her drink, underlining passages in her book, talking to the bartender — who eventually brought her a free dessert — and generally having the most wonderful of solo times, an outing that seemed even better because she was alone. She was alone not just for an experiment, not just because she was hungry, but because this was what she wanted to be doing, right here, right now.

> "I drank my wine and watched her and felt my alone endeavors pale in comparison to hers, until suddenly I realized I was doing exactly the same thing I'd feared others would do to me. I was judging **myself**."

When *Singled Out* was first published in 2006, a reporter wanted to write a story about it for *Cosmo*. She talked to me at length, asked all the right questions, and tried and tried to pitch it. The editors could not be persuaded. So maybe something else has changed over time, and it is not just restaurant diners who are increasingly open to the solo experience.

# 11

# You Are a Badass Because You Like Being Alone with Your Thoughts and Most Other People Can't Stand It

How do you feel about being alone with your own thoughts? Does it sound good to you? It does to me.

Maybe I'm framing that question the wrong way, because in a series of published studies, most people hated it. There were numerous variations in the studies, but all included a quite simple situation: Participants were asked to turn off all their devices, put aside all their stuff (including non-electronic things like pens and papers and books), and just sit with their own thoughts for somewhere between 6 and 15 minutes.

The majority of participants rated the task as difficult and unpleasant. They disliked it whether they did it in a psychology lab or in their own homes. Of those who participated from home, about a third said they cheated by doing things like turning on some music or checking their phones – and those are just the ones who admitted it.

In the flashiest study – the one that's getting the most media attention – participants were asked how they would feel about getting a mild electric shock. Of those who said they would pay *not* to have to experience that, a good number of them went ahead and shocked themselves when left in a room with nothing to do but attend to their own thoughts. (Specifically, 67% of the men and 25% of the women did so.)

Maybe I should rephrase my initial question this way: Just how tethered are you not just to your devices but to every other imaginable distraction, such as watching TV or listening to music or reading or doodling? Do I still stand by my initial reaction that this sort of experience sounds just fine? Do you?

Since reading about the research, I've been thinking of *times when I'm happily lost in my own thoughts*. The situations that first came to mind don't really qualify in the strictest sense, because in each, I'm doing something else at the same time. Here they are:

- When I'm driving, but not when traffic slows to a crawl. (So maybe what's important is choice or a sense of control; it is annoying to be told what to do or to be forced into it by the situation.)

- When I'm cooking.

- When I'm walking or hiking. (I don't like listening to music while I'm out on the trails; it is all about the stimulation of the exercise, the beauty of the settings, and the engagement with my own thoughts.)

- (I'm not a gardener or a knitter or – perhaps most relevant – one who meditates, but I bet people who do engage in those activities enjoy their own thoughts.)

- During boring lectures, I contentedly retreat into my own thoughts for longer periods of time than I want to admit.

- When I'm working (usually writing), I often catch myself looking away from computer screen, staring out the window, and just thinking.

- When I'm traveling by plane, train, or bus. I'm almost always reading but I enjoy taking time to just look out the window and think. That suddenly becomes less enjoyable when, for example, there's an announcement that the flight has been delayed and we'll be sitting on the runway for another half hour. (Again, that suggests the possibility that choice or control may be important.)

- Getting my hair cut. My usual hair stylist is a great conversationalist, but occasionally he is not available and the substitute is much less chatty. When that happens, I retreat into my own thoughts and feel totally contented in doing so.

So, are there any times when I really do just sit with my own thoughts with no other distractions whatsoever? So far, I've come up with two:

- There are times when I'm too tired to work or even read or watch TV, but I'm nowhere near ready to go to sleep. I just need a break. During those times, I like to sit or lounge somewhere comfortable, maybe even close my eyes, and just think.

- Just after my father died (many years ago), there were stretches of time when I did nothing but sit on the couch and stare into space. I'm not sure I did all that much thinking, though, and I'm sure it wasn't pleasant.

It would be useful to conduct diary studies in which people record their daily activities, to see who really does spend time alone with their thoughts.

Maybe we should also start a list of experiences that are less fun than being alone with nothing but your own thoughts. I nominate: getting stuck in a boring group conversation.

In the supplementary materials, the authors list a whole set of factors such demographic characteristics and personality types that they explored, to see whether certain kinds of people enjoy being alone with their thoughts more than others. There were a few significant findings here and there – for example, agreeable people tend to enjoy their own thoughts more – but overall the results were underwhelming.

What struck me about their list was what was missing. My guess is that single people – especially those who are single at heart, and who live alone because they want to, are less allergic to their own thoughts than others. Some, I imagine, actually enjoy them. (Maybe the same is true of only children.) Single people and people who live alone, though, are rarely on the radar of academic psychologists.

# Some People Need to Learn to Be Alone. You, Dear Badass, Are Not One of Them

The title of an intriguing new book, _How to Be Alone_, gives away its goal. The author, Sara Maitland, is out to explain to you, in a smart, insightful, culturally and historically grounded way, how you can come to appreciate solitude, even if you are starting from a place of skepticism and fear.

Maitland is a true believer. Substantial stretches of the book are devoted to the rewards of solitude. She lives in part of Scotland where there is no cell phone service and neighbors are few and far between. If that's all I knew about her, I would have guessed that she is someone who craved time to herself her entire life. But she isn't. She's a solitude convert, having come to the experience after growing up in a big family and then marrying and having kids of her own. She stepped into her post-divorce life with trepidation, but now relishes her time alone.

So, I wonder: Can anyone come to love solitude? Should they try to, even if their initial reaction to the mere thought of spending time alone is repulsion?

The very first page of _How to Be Alone_ includes this:

> "Go into the bathroom; lock the door, take a shower. You are alone.

> "Get in your car and drive somewhere (or walk, jog, bicycle, even swim). You are alone.

> "Wake yourself up in the middle of the night...; don't turn your lights on; just sit in the dark. You are alone."

Her point? Being alone is easy.

She doesn't say so quite yet, but eventually she will try to persuade us that being alone is not just easy, but wonderful. Is there anyone who has not enjoyed taking a long shower or a drive or a walk or a bike ride or a swim?

Solitude, Maitland will maintain, is good for the soul. It is great for creativity; no, it is more than that – it may well be essential. Solitude is freeing. It connects us with nature. It connects us more deeply with ourselves. And, perhaps ironically, having a full measure of solitude is also good for our relationships with other people.

Maitland's suggestions for coming to appreciate solitude more (or, as she puts it, "rebalancing attitudes toward solitude") come in the form of chapter titles:

- "Face the Fear" (she thinks that those who are fearful of solitude should expose themselves to it, 'initially in very low 'doses'")

- "Do Something Enjoyable Alone"

- "Explore Reverie"

- "Look at Nature"

- "Learn Something by Heart" (this was one of the few chapter titles that was not intuitively obvious to me but I got it after reading the chapter)

- "Going Solo" (here she means solo travel and adventures)

- "Train the Children" (for example, we should stop trying to over-schedule our kids and overprotect them from time alone, and we should never use isolation – time outs, going to your room – as punishment)

- "Respect Difference" (This chapter has a great opening line: "Bernard Shaw once said, 'Do not do unto others as you would have them do unto you; they may have very different tastes.'")

I don't know the answer to the question of whether anyone can come to love being alone. I kind of doubt it. But maybe everyone can come to appreciate small samplings of aloneness. Maybe, as the opening page of Maitland's book suggests, they already do but just don't realize it.

The other question I posed is whether people should try to love solitude even if they currently don't like it at all. I'm not so sure about that, either, even though I totally cherish my time alone and arrange to have plenty of it. I do think that young adults, especially, should try spending non-trivial amounts of time alone, for the experience of self-exploration and self-discovery. As for the rest of the adult population – well, I think it is one of the wonders of contemporary life that we have more opportunities than we ever had before to live the way that suits us, whether that is alone, with one other person, or a whole house full of people.

# 13

## Those Poor People Who Are Not Badasses: Time Alone Saps Their Willpower

New research shows that just thinking about spending time alone seems to sap the motivation of people who are neurotic. Compared to when they think about spending time with other people, neurotic individuals can't seem to summon the willpower to persist at tasks such as cleaning the whole house or reading a boring book to the end. Given some anagrams to solve, they solve fewer of them and spend less time trying.

Liad Uziel, a senior lecturer in the psychology at Bar-Ilan University in Israel, authored the article that was published online on July 8, 2016 in the journal *Social Psychological and Personality Science*. He explained that people who are neurotic "experience the world as threatening, problematic, and distressing." Previous research has shown that for neurotic individuals, social life is fraught. They are drawn to other people because of their dependency and their strong need for a sense of belonging. At the same time, they are anxious, negative, and highly sensitive to rejection.

Professor Uziel is one of the few social scientists to ask about the place of solitude in the lives of people high in neuroticism.

For many people, spending time alone can be rewarding, offering opportunities for creativity, relaxation, and unselfconscious absorption in intellectual or spiritual contemplation. Those who savor their solitude often feel refreshed, recharged, and ready to go back out into the world of other people after spending time by themselves. Survey results from the Pew Research Center, based on a representative sample of American adults, showed that more than half said it was very important to be able to spend time completely alone, away from everyone else.

People who are neurotic, however, are unlikely to be among those who value time to themselves. Findings from two German studies showed that neurotic adults scored low on a scale measuring the desire to be alone, endorsing statements such as "Being alone quickly gets to be too much for me."

Does that mean that they are unlikely to feel re-energized after spending time on their own?

In the three studies conducted by Uziel, participants were primed to adopt a mindset about being alone or with other people. Participants got into an alone mindset by repeatedly completing the sentence, "When I am by myself, I..." They got into the social mindset by instead completing the sentence, "When I am in the company of others, I..."

Just thinking about being alone (compared to thinking about being with other people) led the neurotic participants to say that they were much less willing to do activities requiring persistence, patience, and self-control, such as organizing documents or standing in a long line. In two other studies in which they were asked to solve anagrams on a computer, they spent less time working on them and got fewer of them solved. Uziel speculated that without the potential to gain the approval of other people in a social setting, neurotic people just weren't motivated to exert much of an effort.

Uziel focused on the ways in which alone time undermines the motivation of people who are neurotic. His results, though, show something else significant: People who have very few neurotic tendencies seem to thrive when they think about spending time by themselves. Across all three studies, they did at least as well, and sometimes better, when they had an alone mindset than a social one. They expressed a greater willingness to persist at tasks such as standing in a long line or reading an entire boring book. They spent more time on the anagrams task and solved more of them successfully.

For decades, social scientists have been studying the perils of loneliness. Explorations of the potential benefits of solitude are more rare. PsycINFO, the extensive database of research in the social sciences, includes more than 8,000 documents on the topic of loneliness, but fewer than 1,000 about solitude. There is much to be gained by redressing that imbalance. As Uziel noted, it "could provide new understandings of ways toward greater well-being."

# The Positive Psychology of Solitude:
# What's So Great About Being Alone

# The Psychology of Spending Time Alone

How does it feel to spend time alone? What happens, psychologically, when you are by yourself? Does it matter where you are? Who you are?

In one of the earliest studies to address such questions, hundreds of undergraduates were asked about their experiences of being alone – either totally alone or alone in the presence of others (for example, when dining solo). They were asked specifically about nine different ways of experiencing time alone that were found to be important in previous research.

**Which experiences of time alone did people value most?**

When participants rated the importance of each of the nine kinds of solitude experiences (i.e., the amount of effort they would put into having each one; how much each experience had influenced their lives), their rank ordering looked like this:

1. Time alone can be an opportunity to think through your *problems* or the *decisions* you need to make. This was the experience of solitude that participants valued the most.

2. Time alone can be experienced as *inner peace*. You feel relaxed and calm and free of the everyday pressures of your life.

3. Time alone can be good for *self-discovery*. You understand more about your goals and values, strengths and weaknesses.

4. Time alone can be used for *diversions*, such as watching TV, reading, or spending time online.

5. Time alone can awaken your *creativity*. You come up with new ideas, or artistic creations, or intellectual insights.

6. Time alone can offer *freedom from concern about what others think* (**anonymity**). You can do what you want.

7. Time alone can be good for *feeling close to other people* who are not there with you (**intimacy**).

8. Time alone can foster *spirituality*, including closeness to God or a more secular sense of harmony with the world.

9. Time alone can be a time when people experience **loneliness**. Unsurprisingly, the experience of loneliness is valued less than any other way of experiencing solitude.

## Where are people when they have these different experiences of solitude?

Participants were asked whether they were at home, in a public place, or in nature during the various experiences of time alone. All of the experiences, except spirituality, occurred more often at home than anywhere else. For example, when people used their time alone for diversions such as reading, surfing the internet, and watching TV, they were at home 95% of the time. When they experienced time alone as a welcome respite from caring about what others think (anonymity), they were at home 83% of the time.

People most often experienced their time alone as spiritual when they were in nature (67%). The experience of solitude as inner peace also occurred often in nature (42%) though not as often as it occurred when people were at home (53%).

The various experiences of solitude rarely occurred in public places. When people were using their time alone for diversions, they were in public places only 4% of the time. (The study was published in 2003, so it is possible that the number would be higher now that people so often have electronic devices available for entertainment when they are out and about.) Interestingly, the way of experiencing time alone that occurred most often in public places was loneliness. When people were alone in public places, they more often felt loneliness than any of the other experiences.

People almost never used their time alone for diversions when they were in nature. (That happened only 1% of the time.) There was one other experience of solitude that almost never occurred when people were out in nature – loneliness.

## What are the values and personality characteristics associated with different experiences of solitude?

Five of the experiences of solitude are *inner-directed*: inner peace, self-discovery, creativity, freedom from constraints, and thinking through your problems. What values and personality characteristics were associated with valuing those inner-directed experiences of solitude?

Participants were asked about the extent to which they valued power, achievement, hedonism, stimulation, self-direction, universalism, benevolence, tradition, conformity, and security. The people who said that inner-directed experiences of solitude were especially important to them cared most about two values:

*Self-direction*: creativity, curiosity, independence, freedom, choosing one's own goals

*Universalism*: social justice, open-mindedness, peace, equality, nature, the arts, concern with the environment

With regard to their personality characteristics, people who said that inner-directed experiences were especially important to them had these qualities:

*More emotional creativity*: when dealing with challenging situations, they are emotionally adaptive and innovative

*Less depression*

*Less likely to be insecurely attached in an anxious way*

## Some concluding thoughts

There are many positive and enriching ways to experience time alone. Of the nine ways of experiencing time alone, the only wholly negative experience was loneliness. That aversive experience was less commonplace than any other experience, other than spirituality. People were especially unlikely to experience their time alone as lonely when they were in nature.

A very positive profile emerged for the people who especially value inner-directed experiences of solitude (inner peace, self-discovery, creativity, freedom from constraints, and thinking through your problems). They are emotionally creative, unlikely to be depressed, and unlikely to be anxiously attached. They value universalism (e.g., open-mindedness, social justice) and self-direction.

The results are best regarded as suggestive and in need of further study with different kinds of participants. What they suggest, though, is encouraging about what we can get out of the time we spend alone.

**Reference**: Long, C. R., Seburn, M., Averill, J. R., & More, T. A. (2003). Solitude experiences: Varieties, settings, and individual differences. *Personality and Social Psychology Bulletin, 29,* 578-583.

## 15

# The Benefits of Solitude

Many professional researchers have had a hard time recognizing that solitude can actually be beneficial. Maybe part of the reason is that psychologists – especially social psychologists – are particularly attuned to humans as social animals who need and crave connection with other people. In fact, the title of a journal article that has attracted much attention over the years is "The need to belong."

I don't dispute the social needs of humans. I just don't see them as incompatible with an appreciation for solitude. To get a sense of psychologists struggling with the notion that time alone can actually be a *good* thing, consider these two examples of titles of journal articles:

- "When the need to belong goes wrong"

- "Finding pleasure in solitary activities: desire for aloneness or disinterest in social contact?"

Titles such as these seem to suggest that if you spend time alone, there must be something wrong with you. Maybe your need to belong has "gone wrong." Maybe you don't really want to be alone, you are just anxious and avoiding other people. But that's not what the studies show. Some people really do want their time alone and regard it as something positive and constructive; they are not skittishly fleeing scary humans.

In a study of fifth through ninth graders, Reed Larson found that over time, the older children choose to spend more time alone. What's more, their emotional experience was improved after they had spent some time on their own. Those adolescents who spent an intermediate amount of time alone – not too much, not too little – seemed to be doing the best psychologically.

Two psychologists who really do get it about the sweetness of solitude are Christopher Long and James Averill. The title of their key theoretical article is "Solitude: An exploration of the benefits of being alone." No apology. No befuddlement that humans might actually benefit from their time alone.

Here's how they characterize solitude:

> "The paradigm experience of solitude is a state characterized by disengagement from the immediate demands of other people – a state of reduced social inhibition and increased freedom to select one's mental and physical activities."

Although there can be benefits to spending time with others, there can also be rewards to "disengagement from the immediate demands of other people."

There is research (again by Larson) in which people are beeped at random times during the day and asked about their experiences. Unsurprisingly, people report feeling less self-conscious when they are alone than when they are with others.

Other than the welcome emotional respite, what's so good about feeling less self-conscious? Long and Averill think that it is good for creativity. They note findings from other research showing that adolescents who can't deal with being alone are less likely to develop their creative abilities.

The theme that resonates most with me is the argument that other people can be distracting and taxing. I'm not talking specifically about being with people who are annoying and demanding. Instead, the idea is that just having other people around – even wonderful other people – can sap some of your cognitive and emotional resources. You might, even at some very low level, use up some of your psychological energy wondering about their needs and concerns, or considering the impression you may be making on them (even if you are not insecure about that), or maybe even just sensing their presence when you are sharing the same space and not even conversing.

There is a freedom that comes with solitude, and (as Long and Averill note) it is both a freedom from constraints and a positive freedom to do what you want and let your thoughts wander. Here's another quote from them that I especially appreciate, as it showcases their perspective that spending time alone and getting something out of it can be a strength, rather than a cause for concern:

> "the (positive) *freedom to* engage in a particular activity requires more than simply a *freedom from* constraint or interference: it also requires the resources or capacity to use solitude constructively."

Antarctic researchers, who have chosen a pursuit that requires spending a lot of time alone, score especially high on a scale measuring "absorption." The scale assesses enjoyment of experiences such as watching clouds in the sky, and becoming particularly absorbed in a movie you are watching.

In solitude, Long and Averill suggest, we sometimes think about ourselves and our priorities in new ways. Our thinking about other matters, too, may be more likely to be transformed during times of solitude.

The particular intersection of solitude and single life – like so many other aspects of solitude – has yet to be studied in any detail. My guess is that people who are single – especially if they are single at heart – like their solitude more than people who crave coupling do. I'll end with one more quote from Long and Averill. They were not discussing single people when they said it, but it strikes me as relevant:

> "...cognitive transformation can be threatening rather than liberating. At the very least, in order to benefit from solitude, the individual must be able to draw on inner resources to find meaning in a situation in which external supports are lacking."

### References:

Long, C. R., & Averill, J. R. (2003). Solitude: An exploration of the benefits of being alone. *Journal for the Theory of Social Behavior, 33*, 21-44.

Larson, R. W. (1997). The emergence of solitude as a constructive domain of experience in early adolescence. *Child Development, 68*, 80-93.

# 16

# Another Great Thing About Being Alone

Rest. How great does that sound? In our harried times, many crave it. Yet for a long time, we've known little about it. We never knew the answers to basic questions as: What feels restful? Who gets enough rest and who doesn't? Does it really matter?

The wellness company, Hubbub, wanted to know more. Together with BBC radio presenter Claudia Hammond, they brought together collaborators from twelve disciplines to design The Rest Test. The online survey drew 18,000 participants from 134 countries. That made it the biggest study of rest by far, though the participants were self-selected and not a representative sample of any of the nations.

Rather than defining rest, the researchers asked the participants to choose the three activities, from a list of 25, that they found most restful. *The activities most often experienced as restful were the kinds of things most often done alone.*

### Activities Most Often Experienced as Restful

These activities were described as most restful by more than 50% of the participants:

- Reading

- Being in the natural environment

- Spending time alone

These activities were mentioned as especially restful by somewhere between about 35% and 41% of the participants:

- Listening to music

- Doing nothing in particular

- Walking

- Having a bath or shower

- Daydreaming

- Watching TV

Finally, these activities were selected as particularly restful by somewhere between about 22% and 26% of the participants:

- Meditating or practicing mindfulness

- Being with animals

- Seeing friends or family

- Drinking tea or coffee

- Doing creative arts

- Gardening

Other research shows that we are particularly happy when we are hanging out with our friends. This research suggests that a happy experience is not necessarily a restful one – seeing friends and family ranks fairly low on the list of restful experiences. The researchers had data on participants' levels of extroversion and found that even for the extroverts, the kinds of activities they could do on their own were considered more restful than spending time with other people.

One activity that did not make the list of most restful activities was *exercise*. Even so, a nontrivial group of people – 16 percent – said that they found exercise restful.

### How Much Rest Do People Get and How Much Do They Wish They Could Get?

Participants were asked how much rest they got in the past 24 hours. Again, they got to define rest for themselves. Answers ranged from none to 14 hours. The average was about 3 hours.

Was that enough? Two-thirds said no: They would like to get more rest.

Among the *least rested* people were:

- People with high incomes
- People working night shifts
- People with full-time jobs
- People who were caring for others

Among the *most rested* people were:

- Older people
- Retired people
- Unemployed people
- People with lower incomes

Most people with full-time jobs said that rest was the opposite of work. People who were self-employed and people who did volunteer work were less likely to see rest as the opposite of work. We don't know for sure why that it, but maybe it is because self-employed people and volunteers are more likely to be doing work they find meaningful. They probably also have more control over when (and maybe even where) they work – that probably feels restful, too.

In some circles, there is a kind of status to claiming to be super busy. Maybe some people underestimate the amount of rest they get in order to seem more impressive. For example, the researchers reported that the men, more often than the women, said that they got less rest than the average person. But when the researchers looked at the reports of how much rest the participants had actually gotten in the previous 24 hours, the men had gotten more rest than the women.

## What Does Rest Feel Like?

If you think that the question, "What does rest feel like?", is a silly or obvious one, then you may well have an enviably uncomplicated relationship with rest. You are probably among the majority of people who say that rest feels "relaxing," "peaceful/calming", "comfortable," or "recuperative."

Not everyone feels that way. For 9 percent of the participants in the study, the idea of rest is associated with darker experiences such as "guilty" and "stress-inducing."

Participants were also asked what goes on in their minds when they are on their own. Most often, they said they were focused on their feelings. They said they were carrying on an inner dialog with themselves about 30 percent of the time.

## Does It Matter If You Get Enough Rest?

Participants answered questions about their well-being (for example, having more positive feelings and fewer negative ones). The researchers correlated those scores with participants' reports of how much time they had spent resting during the previous 24 hours.

Generally, people who had more rest experienced greater well-being. Extra hours of rest increased well-being all the way up to about 5 or 6 hours. After that, well-being slipped a little, but still remained high.

Because these are just correlations, we don't know whether getting more rest makes people happier, or whether happier people get more rest, or whether something else about particular people makes them both happier and more likely to get rest.

The researchers also compared the people who said they did not need any more rest than they were already getting to those who wished they could get more rest. They found that "people who don't feel in need of more rest have well-being scores twice as high as those who feel they need more rest."

## Conclusion

Here's how the authors summarized their conclusion:

"To truly feel rest do we need time alone without fear of interruption, when we can be alone with our thoughts? From the Rest Test, it would appear so."

# What's So Great About Solitude?
# People Who Are "Single at Heart" Explain

In the "single at heart" survey, people who described themselves as "single at heart" – they live their best lives by living single – indicated in their own words why they consider themselves to be single at heart. They gave lots of different kinds of answers. Many emphasized the importance of time alone.

Below are some sample quotes. More than half of the participants who talked about the importance of solitude said that they liked it and enjoyed it. Some went further – they said they did not just like their solitude, they *needed* it. Others focused as much or more on having their own space as having time to themselves.

Some participants noted that they like their solitude but also valued spending time with other people. Others said that the time they spend with other people is just not as fulfilling as the time they spend on their own.

Don't stop reading too soon, because in the last category you will find examples of some of the thoughtful explanations of just why solitude is so important to some of the people who see themselves as single-at-heart.

## QUOTES ABOUT SOLITUDE FROM THE SURVEY: PARTICIPANTS' OWN WORDS

A. **I like it, I enjoy it:**

1. I like my own company.

2. I enjoy being on my own.

3. It's been this way my whole life, ever since I can remember, I have always enjoyed alone time.

4. I just prefer to be alone and/or have complete control over the amount of time I spend interacting with other people.

5. I enjoy my own time, my personal space, dinner by myself even.

6. I love my time alone

7. Even though I am married, I am happiest when I am on my own for personal time.

8. I like solitude, like doing things by myself.

9. I genuinely enjoy spending quiet time with my own thoughts.

10. I don't feel lonely when I am alone.

11. I love being alone (I'm actually never really alone because I always have my own company!) and only once in a while feel lonely.

B. I **need** it:

1. My time alone is as essential to my being a functional human being as food is.

2. I need my own time and space!

3. Even when I find a potential partner, I find myself preferring to be alone. As much as some people NEED to be in relationships and can't function alone, others of us need to have our own space and not be tied to one person for our day to day lives.

4. I always felt happy living alone, but until I moved in with friends I did not realize how important it was to me to live alone! I look forward to nothing as much as I look forward to snuggling up in my room, alone with a good book and my favorite music playing. And I have started daydreaming constantly about moving out and once more being on my own entirely.

5. I require significant time alone.

6. When I was younger I didn't understand why I just enjoyed me and pets.

7. I need and enjoy of my personal time.

8. I need more time to myself than the average person.

C. **Importance of my own space:**

1. When I get home, I want it to be my space.

2. I would much rather live in my own space all the time, with occasional partners to spice things up.

3. Even if I found a man willing to pick up after himself, I would still want my own place to go to and get away from a romantic partner sometimes.

D. **I like time alone and time with others, too:**

1. I like my solitude, and know that if I want company I can always go out or call a friend.

2. I love being alone. I have lots of friends. Being alone is not equal to being lonely!

3. I like being with myself. When I want company I seek it out. And I am content with that.

4. I'm very sociable but also like to have my space.

5. I'm married but I like doing things that I enjoy doing alone or with friends.

E. **Time with other people is just not as fulfilling as time alone:**

1. I genuinely prefer to be alone and or with my dogs. When I go to parties I spend time thinking that I could be at home reading and or watching TV. I love the quiet of solitude.

2. No one I meet is nearly as interesting to me as anything I could read in a technical or research book.

3. While I can imagine a relationship structured in a way that I could enjoy, I'm not sure even that would make me happier or more fulfilled than I am alone.

4. My friends asked why I didn't find a guy here in town. My gut answer: because I don't want him always around!

5. I've always felt that after coming home from work, if I had to have someone else around and think about them and how they felt it would be exhausting to me. Actually, I simply wouldn't care; nor would I want anyone else there.

## F. **Here's what solitude does for me:**

1. I feel the most "centered" and at peace when I am alone.

2. I appreciate the peacefulness of a solitary existence.

3. I need the solitude to rejuvenate for work. I like the quiet and contemplation to feel whole and complete.

4. I absolutely need solitude, to regain my power and find room for my own thoughts.

5. I love being with myself alone. I'm happy going to a restaurant, a movie, the zoo, a museum on my own. I'm never bored. I have more to give both myself and others when I take care of my own personal space and self.

6. I have always enjoyed my own company. I have felt VERY alone at times when in a relationship. I am at my most authentic when doing things, I enjoy on my own.

7. Although I love to be social and spend time with friends, I find a little social time goes a long way – I like to spend the vast majority of my time alone, and another person in the house, even if they're not talking to me or interacting with me directly at the moment, seems to take up a lot of my emotional energy. I can only really relax and be creative when I'm on my own. I love travel ling alone, living alone – as long as I have a few good friends to hang out with now and then, I'm never lonely.

# 18

# The Deep Rewards of a Deeply Single Life

"I want to be in an exclusive relationship with myself." That's how writer Ann Friedman described her desire, around the age of 30, to put an end to her life of being someone's girlfriend for far too many years.

She chose to spend the next years in a state she called "deep single," in which dating was infrequent and repeat-dating with the same person was even more rare. "Those years were, hands down, the most professionally productive and fulfilling of my life," she tells us in an essay in *Marie Claire*.

When people who have never really craved the "deeply single" experience try to imagine the appeal, they often come up with things like, you get to arrange your place the way you want it and eat what you want whenever you want. Those can be perks of living single, especially if you are single and also live alone (not all singles do). Friedman described some of the delights of arranging her place and her things the way she wanted them, and not the way she had settled on with boyfriends. When you make your own home, you get to savor it every day of your life, so the matter is not totally trivial.

Yet what the couple-minded don't fully recognize are the deeper ways in which a deeply single life can be satisfying. Here are some of the more profound satisfactions of deeply single life that Friedman described:

1. She pursued the professional opportunities that were most meaningful to her, whether that meant leaving D.C. or moving to Texas or moving a month later to Los Angeles

2. "With only me to stop me, I was unstoppable."

3. Her social life expanded (consistent with tons of research). Instead of spending all her time with the same social group that she and her boyfriend had ossified in, she nurtured her connections with several circles of friends.

4. She got to spend "a lot of quality time alone." For people who love their single lives, <u>alone time</u> is rarely frightening or even boring; it is more often profoundly satisfying.

5. "Being single doesn't just make you more independent: It makes you more interesting."

Friedman also became a bit less pliant about the "poor-me, I'm-single" conversations that went on around her. She just would not participate in them anymore. Having sampled the deep satisfactions of deeply single life, she found it "excruciating to hear women talk about how desperate they are to be in a relationship—any relationship." Ann Friedman liked truth better than clichés, and the truth she discovered was that "your 'real life' doesn't begin when you meet a partner. It's happening now."

There is something else Friedman mentioned, which grabbed me not because it counts as one of the deepest rewards of single life, but because it is a metaphor for single life that <u>one person after another finds attractive and apt</u>: She and her best friend drove along the coast, "a vacation we'd fantasized about for years." Open road, vast ocean views—something about that says "single" in a fundamentally positive way.

I love how beautifully Friedman articulated the profound appeal of a deeply single life, but I'm not so sure she is <u>single at heart</u>. She talks about those deeply single years as if they are in the past, so perhaps they are. Maybe her experiences suggest something else important about the single-at-heart experience. Maybe it is not just something enduring about a person, like a personality trait. Perhaps for some people, living the deeply single life is something that is tremendously appealing for years, but not for a lifetime. We have so much more to learn about what single-at-heart really means.

# 19

# Are There Times When You Want to Be Alone, But No One Else Understands?

On the day my father died very suddenly, many years ago, my mother called two of my close friends before she called me. She wanted me to have someone with me after I heard the news.

Eventually, I would very much appreciate the company and comfort of my friends. But I did not want to see them right after hearing such devastating news. I just wanted to be alone.

I don't know how unusual I am in wanting to be alone a lot of the time, including times when many other people would crave the presence of others. I do know there are others who share this preference – for example, from conversations in Community of Single People. I just don't know how common we are.

Part of the problem is that the kinds of people who want to be with other people much of the time are the people who get the most attention. Their stories are told and retold, and in that way, normalized. Maybe I didn't say as much as I do now about my own preferences for time alone, and as a result, back then, even my own mother did not realize how I would want to process such devastating news.

For me, it is not just during bad times, but also some good ones, that I savor my solitude. That, too, can be hard for people to fathom. When I lived on the East Coast, I used to rent a beach house for a week or two every year in the little town of Duck on the Outer Banks of North Carolina. I invited friends or family to join me for some of the time, but I always wanted a few days alone. I just loved having the house and all those hours all to myself. It is a whole different experience from vacationing with others – which I also loved.

It was difficult to maintain my claim on those couple of days that I wanted to be alone. One year, when I invited my parents to come on the second day of my rental, they surprised me and arrived on the first day. They thought I'd be thrilled. They meant well, so I never told them I wasn't. Another year, I invited my friends for the all the days except the last two. When it came time for my friends to leave, one of them didn't understand (even though I was clear when I invited her). She asked me if she could stay for the last two days. I found a way to say no, but I felt terrible about it.

I've heard from other people that they have had similar experiences. They, too, feel very badly about telling people whose company they like a lot that there are times when they don't want their company, not even to do fun things.

Too bad we end up feeling badly about wanting time to ourselves. Maybe if we talk more often and more openly about our preferences, things will begin to change. The people who get rebuffed will know that they shouldn't take it personally, and the people who do the rebuffing won't feel guilty.

# 20

# Home Alone:
# What the Gilmore Girls Got Right

On the TV show, Th Gilmore Girls, mother Lorelai Gilmore and daughter Rory are a single-parent family that shines. I enjoy the friendship and love between them, and the passion each of them has for her work (paid work for mom and school work for daughter). Rory is super smart, gets absorbed in books to the point of obliviousness to everything else around her, and wants to go to Harvard. And she makes no apologies for any of that. In fact, she seems utterly joyful and unselfconscious about her love of learning.

In what may be my favorite episode so far, Lorelai is going to be away for the evening and Rory is so happy just to be able to spend the evening home alone. Her plans are nothing dramatic. She just wants to do the laundry her own way, order tons of the food she likes the best, and, best of all, simply have the house to herself.

None of her peers can understand this. Her boyfriend is flabbergasted that the two of them could have the place to themselves, but Rory wants to stay home alone – to do laundry! Another guy who is interested in Rory makes up an excuse and a lie to stop by – then doesn't want to leave. Paris, Rory's competitive friend from school, is freaking out about her less than perfect grade on a recent test, and keeps whining and begging Rory to let her come by to study, until finally, when she appears at the door, Rory caves. Rory does insist, though, that Paris can only stay for an hour, then she has to leave. Of course, Rory eventually gives up on that, too.

Nothing works. Rory doesn't get her luxurious night to spend home alone, and none of her friends ever really gets it about the attraction of such an evening.

But I get it. And I suspect that many other people do, too – perhaps especially those who are single at heart. I've had the same sort of yearning and craving all my life. I grew up in a household with three siblings and two parents and a stream of aunts and uncles and cousins and friends dropping by all the time. There was just one time when the house was likely to be empty – early in the evenings on Sundays. I savored those times, and I never did anything more exciting than Rory did.

So, thank you, Gilmore Girls, for airing a version of Home Alone that really hit home for me. We need more recognition that spending time alone with nothing special to do is not necessarily boring or lonely. For some of us, it is deeply satisfying.

# 21

# A Story of Single Life You Haven't Heard Before

I love my single life. I never needed to learn to love it – that came naturally. I'm single-at-heart.

I realize, though, that the same is not true for all other single people. I like reading about their experiences, too, especially if they are good writers.

J. Victoria Sanders is a very engaging writer. Once I started reading her book, _Single & Happy: The Party of Ones_, I just kept going. That was so even though, in many ways, I could not relate. For example, a chapter title, "Is it impossible to be single and happy?", creates no suspense for me. I know the answer. Yet I was totally absorbed in reading about the author's answer.

I don't need tips for learning to appreciate solitude; I love solitude. Yet, I enjoyed reading and contemplating Victoria Sanders's recommendations:

- "Get a good book, or a few..."

- "Dedicate one day a week to eating whatever you want..."

- "Play your favorite music as loudly as you want..."

- "Schedule random massages..."

- "Exercise..."

- "Garden or find another soothing, life-affirming hobby..."

- "Find a useless hobby..."

As much as I savor my solitude, there are some ways in which the author is even better at it than I am. Consider this quote:

*"Except for when I go to the theater with one or two of my introverted friends, I mostly really, really love being in a theater with no one sitting next to me fussing about popcorn or complaining about the previews and the ads or whatever."*

I have gone to movies on my own, but true confession: I don't really like it. If I'm going to watch a movie on my own, I'd rather be on my comfy couch where I can hit pause and go get some popcorn that will not cost me all my lunch money.

I have thought a lot about the value of solitude and what it offers, but I never came up with this point that Sanders made:

*"As much as I love being connected to others, constant contact makes it easy for me to get wrapped up in other people's lives and start comparing myself to people I don't even want to be like."*

In the title of this post, I claimed that this story of single life is one that you have not heard before. In a way, every single person's story is one you have not heard before, but in Sanders' case, there is a particularly poignant theme: She spent much of her childhood homeless. She and her mom (who had mental health issues) moved often, from shelter to shelter. She believes that her itinerant childhood made her even more reliant than most on popular media in order to figure out big-picture lessons about relationships, single life, and life. The enduring sets of family members and friends and role models of various sorts that are part of the childhoods of so many kids were not part of hers.

Because of her experiences, Sanders's take on media portrayals of single life and of the self-help juggernaut is particularly telling. I took in her observations in a way that is a bit different from how I digest other articles and books and blogs.

What Victoria Saunders has done with her life is special, too. Hats off to "Single & Happy."

# Why Whoopi Goldberg Doesn't Want Anyone to Complete Her

If someone says, 'You complete me,' RUN!" That's the title of a book by Whoopi Goldberg. It is one of the many wise things she learned from a lifetime of experiences and now wants to share with her readers.

I think Whoopi Goldberg is single at heart but she sure has not spent her whole life single. As she explains:

"I thought that in order to be 'normal,' I had to be married. So I got married even though I knew it wasn't right. When that didn't work out I tried it again. And then again."

Whoopi believes you need to know who you are and be honest with yourself and other people about that. Then you need to live that life that is right for you, and not the life that other people expect you to live or try to shame you into living.

Whoopi also wants you to understand those romantic songs and movies and even many commercials for what they are – fantasies and mythologies, not real life. "We think these movies give us hope," she cautions, "but in reality they just create false expectations that will come back and bite us in the butt." Same for the love songs. For example, Whoopi has an answer to the question posed by the Supremes, "Where Would I Be Without You?" Her answer: "Hopefully still yourself."

One of the things I appreciated most about the book was something that is all too rare: Whoopi not only proclaims that she is not interested in coupling up, she recognizes that there are others who are not interested in that, either. She also affirms that there are other kinds of relationships and other kinds of love, in addition to the romantic variety.

Here are some of my favorite quotes.

## On Living Single

*"I need you to understand that it is okay to want to be by yourself."*

What Whoopi thinks you should be doing: *"...leading your own fulfilling life, learning new things, working on your career, your friends and family, your causes and passions. Instead of sitting around waiting for some guy to call, go develop yourself."*

*"The idea* [that you need] *to find someone and couple up...makes people who are not interested in coupling up, or who at this point in their lives are not coupled up, feel terrible. It makes us ask ourselves, 'Is there something wrong with me? Why doesn't someone want me?'"*

*"You should be able to do things for yourself, no matter how big or how small. You should be able to make yourself happy."*

Sometimes people want to live single because of things such as the ones Whoopi describes, including *"I don't have to talk to anyone if I don't feel like it"* and *"I can hear my own thoughts."* She concludes: *"This freedom for me is worth far more than any relationship."*

## Bad Reasons to Couple Up

*"People tend to rush into relationships because they are afraid they are not going to have anybody, like that's a bad thing."*

*"No one should feel like they have to have someone there with them to show outside people that they're worthy. It takes a solid person who knows who she is to go to the dinner party by herself and hold her own."*

If you want a partner *"because they can do stuff for you, or because they will take care of you financially, that is not a good enough reason. All the things on your checklist of what you want him to be – you'd better equal them...Take responsibility for yourself, and don't expect someone else to do it for you."*

Same for men: *"Learn to do stuff on your own."* (And no, Whoopi is not just writing for straight people.)

<u>Why you should run if you hear, "You complete me":</u>

- *"If they complete you, they can deconstruct you as well."*

- *"It is almost like you don't have enough sense to do sh\*t on your own."*

- *"...the idea that we are walking around as half a person, I find bizarre."*

Don't get married:

- *"because you're lonely"*

- *"to prove a point"*

- *"to get back at somebody"*

- *"because your mother wants you to"*

- *"because you figure, 'What the hell'"*

## On Bigger, Broader Meanings of Family, Relationships, Love, and Soul Mates

*"I believe in soul mates but I don't believe that you have to have sex with your soul mate or marry your soul mate...I have four soul mates now. They are people for whom I would give my life. But I wouldn't have them come live with me in my house. I don't want to marry them. They are married to other people anyway."*

*"...family just means you're related by blood – but sometimes there are other families that are better suited for you, more than the one you were born into."*

*"One of the things that everyone seems to do when they find a new partner is they disappear...This is a terrible thing. It's wonderful to fall in love and go into your love cave for a little while, but you can't just disappear from the friends who have been there for you all along. That's so high school."*

*"...people don't understand that friendships sometimes are the things that last longest in life."*

*"If you have dear friends, they are the people that make your soul whole."*

# Time Alone:
# Craving It More Than Ever

# 23

# The American Psyche:
# Tipping Toward Solitude?

I live in the most ordinary American household - I live alone. Knock on any door in the nation and you are more likely to find a household like mine than a household with mom, dad, and the kids, or a household with a married couple and no kids, or a single-parent household, or any other kind.

There has been a surge in the number of single-person households, and a decline in the number of married-with-kids households. This is not a fad - it is a decades-long demographic juggernaut. It has many pundits and prognosticators plenty worried.

One of their fears is that we may be on the cusp of an epidemic of loneliness. Interventions, they say, may be in order. Some even present statistics in support of the link between living alone and feeling lonely. Not bogus statistics but real ones. For example, a recent report about the well-being of older people in the UK noted that 17% of older people living alone say that they are often lonely, compared to only 2% of those living with others.

That's a meaningful difference. I do believe that many older people are isolated, lonely, and depressed (though not as many as our stereotypes would lead us to believe). Their problems should be taken seriously. But let's not make a pathology out of a preference.

Think again about the statistic that 17% of older people living alone report that they often feel lonely. What strikes me about this finding is that 83% of older people living alone do NOT often feel lonely. Remember that they are old, some may have health problems that limit their mobility, others may have close friends and family who have died, and they are living without anyone under the same roof readily available for small talk or interesting excursions. Yet 83% say that they are not often lonely.

When I was writing *Singled Out*, I read voraciously about demographic patterns (such as the increase in 1-person households) and about loneliness, and thought a lot about my own life. I live alone and I am almost never lonely. I am also rarely bored. Then I realized something that seemed startling at first: During those atypical times when I am bored, I am almost always with other people. I'm never bored when I'm alone.

I don't consider myself a total introvert. I love to socialize (with people who do not bore me), I love the visits (time-limited) from friends and family who come to catch up with me and soak up the sun from my deck, and I love to entertain. But I also cherish my solitude.

## Introverts and loners: They are not apologizing anymore

Jonathan Rauch does consider himself an introvert. In 2003, he wrote an essay for the *Atlantic* magazine that began like this:

Do you know someone who *needs hours alone every day*? Who loves quiet conversations about feelings or ideas, and can give a dynamite presentation to a big audience, but seems awkward in groups and maladroit at small talk? Who has to be dragged to parties and then needs the rest of the day to recuperate? Who growls or scowls or grunts or winces when accosted with pleasantries by people who are just trying to be nice?

If so, do you tell this person he is 'too serious,' or ask if he is okay? Regard him as aloof, arrogant, rude? Redouble your efforts to draw him out?

If you answered yes to these questions, chances are that you have an introvert on your hands - and that you aren't caring for him properly.

Rauch, a prolific writer, got more enthusiastic responses to that essay than to anything else he had ever written. Three years later, the *Atlantic* reported that readers were still clicking their approval: Online, no other piece had drawn more traffic than Rauch's "Caring for Your Introvert."

The same year that Rauch's essay appeared, the witty and wonderful *Party of One: The Loners' Manifesto* was also published. Loners, notes author Anneli Rufus, are people who prefer to be alone. They are not sad, lonely, or deranged.

Contrary to stereotypes and TV-punditry, loners are not serial murderers and they are not school shooters, either. True, there are criminals who look like loners, in that they spend lots of time alone. Typically, though, they are just pseudo-loners, who never craved all that time to themselves. They wanted to be included but were instead rejected.

True loners do not withdraw in order to stew in misery or plot violent revenge. Instead, Rufus reminds us, loners "know better than anyone how to entertain themselves...They have a knack for imagination, concentration, inner discipline, and invention."

Not all introverts or loners live alone. Their experiences, though, should give pause to those whose thoughts leap to loneliness when imagining the experiences of solo-dwellers, and to those who are tempted to swoop in with their interventions to rescue people who may be perfectly content exactly as they are.

## Togetherness can also breed loneliness

The same report that underscored a link between living alone and feeling lonely also implicated divorce in the mix. As one headline put it, "Easy divorce has left elderly lonely and depressed."

The logic is that people who are divorced, and who also feel lonely, are lonely because they are divorced. Probably a good number really are.

The reverse sequence, though, should not be discounted. Some people divorce because they are lonely in their marriages. In the anthology, _Women on Divorce_, several contributors described such experiences. Ann Hood, for example, said, "I wanted my old pre-marriage back...I remembered how at night I used to sleep well. How being alone felt fine because there was no one down the hall not talking to me." Daphne Merkin added, "I, for instance, married a man who left me feeling lonely not because he wasn't home but because he was."

## Preferences for togetherness can change over time

When I arrived at my first academic job at the age of 26, I considered it my great good fortune to have colleagues who wanted to go out to lunch every day. Now, decades later, if I had to go out to lunch every day - even with people I really like - I would go stark raving mad.

Early theorists of aging believed that with age came isolation. Some thought that older people were socially marginalized by a society preoccupied with youth. Others believed that older people wanted to withdraw from society, so they isolated themselves on purpose.

Then along came Laura Carstensen and her colleagues, who actually studied the social interaction preferences of people of different ages. Carstensen found that older people socialize more selectively. They still spend time with the people to whom they feel closest. They don't bother as much, though, with people they do not know so well, or with people who annoy them. That's by choice.

## Tipping toward solitude

If there is such a thing as a national psyche, then I think the American version is showing signs of change. Think of trends such as the growing number of people who live alone, the growing preference for working from home, the increasing inclination for families (who have the means to do so) to give their kids rooms of their own, and the preference for older people to live independently as long as possible (instead of moving in with other family members, as they once did). There are many possible reasons for each of these trends, but perhaps at least some of the people in each of the categories have one thing in common: They like their time alone.

In all of our lives, we negotiate a balance between the time we spend with others and the time we spend alone. There are, and always will be, big individual differences. Some love the constant give-and-take of the company of other people, and others prefer more alone time.

Of course, humans are social beings. Meaningful relationships with other people, and time spent with others, will always be important. Still, if there were a national average of the solitude-sociability balance, and if that average were computed over time, I bet it would show that the American scales are tipping toward solitude.

# What's the #1 Source of Joy in the Lives of 25-to-39-Year-Olds?

The age at which people think of themselves as adults has been creeping upward, to the extent that a new stage of development has been added to the familiar ones such as childhood, adolescence, and adulthood. "Emerging adulthood," the term coined by social scientist Jeffrey Arnett, refers to those years when people are no longer adolescents but not quite established as adults either. (Other monikers have also been used, such as "adultolescents.") Somewhere between 25 and 39, though, the majority of people feel that they have reached adulthood.

So, what then? How do people feel about their lives during those early years of making it to adulthood? That's what Arnett set out to explore in a national survey of a diverse sample of more than 1,000 Americans between the ages of 25 and 39.

In his sample, 51 percent were married, 12 percent were cohabiting, and 10 percent had a close boyfriend or girlfriend. He classified as single the other 27% (though legally, 49 percent were single).

When asked to indicate their current sources of enjoyment, which of the following do you think was mentioned most often? I'll list the possibilities alphabetically so you can test your intuition:

- Exercise or playing sports

- Having time to myself

- Hobbies or leisure activities

- Pets

- Relationships with friends

- Relationships with parents

- Relationships with siblings

- Travel or holidays

- Using social media

- Watching television

If you guessed "having time to myself," you are right! Here is the same list of 10 possible sources of enjoyment (the 10 that were mentioned by more than half of all participants), this time ordered by the percent of people who endorsed each:

- 91%, having time to myself

- 86%, hobbies or leisure activities

- 83%, relationships with friends

- 82%, travel or holidays

- 79%, watching television

- 77%, relationships with parents

- 76%, using social media

- 66%, exercising or playing sports

- 65%, relationships with siblings

- 55%, pets

When reporting that "having time to myself" came out on top, Arnett and his coauthor Joseph Schwab speculated that time to oneself may be especially valuable because it is so rare. One of their other results seems consistent with that possibility. When asked to indicate their main sources of stress, the 25-39-year-olds most often mentioned "too much to do and not enough time to do it all" (64 percent; next in line was financial stress, mentioned by 60 percent).

I suspect that the time crunch explanation is only part of the story. In my preliminary research on people who are, and are not, single at heart, I found that just about everyone who identifies as "single at heart" feels very positively about having time alone. The key question in my survey is, *"When you think about spending time alone, what thought comes to mind first?"* Alternatives were "Ah, sweet solitude" and "Oh, no, I might be lonely!" Among people who are most clearly single-at-heart, 99 percent of them (!) chose "Ah, sweet solitude." But even among those who are most clearly not single-at-heart, more than half (56 percent) also chose the sweet solitude answer. So maybe having too much to do and not enough time to do it all exacerbates the craving for time to yourself, but I think you can savor that alone-time even if you are not feeling stressed.

# What Does the Richest Person in the World Want?

When researching _How We Live Now: Redefining Home and Family in the 21st Century_, I spent several years traveling around the country asking people to let me into their homes and their lives. One of the themes that emerged from my interviews and other research is that everyone wants some mixture of time alone and time with other people, but the ideal proportion varies wildly from one person to the next. If there is one overall trend, though, I think it is that on the average, people today want more time and space to themselves than they wanted in the past. A great example is the story of Bill Gates. I wish I could say that I interviewed him personally, but alas, this account comes from what I found in other articles.

The richest person in the world lives in a 66,000 square-foot mansion. Bill Gates could probably find some space to claim as his alone anytime he so wishes. Still, his house does not seem to afford him all the solitude his heart desires. Twice a year, he boards a seaplane or helicopter to a modest lakeside cottage for Think Week. (The specific location is kept secret.) His wife, his kids, the Microsoft people, and all other humans are banned from the cottage. The person who delivers meals is the sole exception. At his private retreat, Gates reads, works, walks the beach, stays up as long as he wants, and sleeps whenever he feels like it.

Is the legendary Think Week just some random anecdote? Or is it part of a more sweeping trend in which people who can afford to buy anything in the world choose solitude? And many others with far less money use what they do have to lay claim to a place that is theirs alone? And even those who live with others stake out a bedroom or a bathroom or a shed as their own private space? If we could map relative preferences for sociability vs. solitude over the years, I think we would find that the American psyche is tipping toward solitude.

# What Does the Most Powerful Person in the World Want?

*August, 2016.* [Barack Obama was President.]

Perhaps no person anywhere has more responsibilities, more power, or more burdens than the President of the United States. Barack Obama gets precious little sleep. At the end of the day, when there are no more meetings on his calendar, when he's already had dinner, and – except for the stack of briefing papers – his time is his own, what does he want to do with his time?

I know what I'd want to do: sleep. That's what President George W. Bush chose: He was usually in bed by 10 pm. President Bill Clinton liked to stay up late and talk on the phone with friends and fellow political types into the wee hours. President Obama is a late-night person, too. But he craves time to himself. Four or five hours to himself. He reads (always those 10 letters from ordinary Americans he reads every evening, always briefing papers, sometimes novels), maybe works on a speech, sometimes with ESPN on in the background.

He could skim some time off the reading for pleasure or watching sports, and instead get a bit more sleep. It is not as if he doesn't crave sleep – he looks forward to getting a whole lot more once he leaves the White House. But he seems to savor his solitude even more. That's what I learned from the *New York Times* article, "Obama after dark: The precious hours alone."

What the most powerful person in the world wants is time alone.

Researchers in psychology have been obsessed with loneliness. Go to the database of all psychology publications, PsycINFO, and type in "loneliness" and you will get more than 8,000 results. Type in "solitude" and you will get fewer than 1,000. Loneliness is a serious matter and deserves research attention. But solitude is significant, too. The research and theory available so far suggests that the rewards of spending time alone, for those who are open to them, include creativity, relaxation, restoration, spirituality, and personal growth.

President Obama, of course, is married, and many married people cherish some time to themselves. My guess, though, is that single people are even more likely to value their time alone. My preliminary research on people who are "single at heart" shows that they embrace their alone time. When asked how they feel when they have some time to themselves on the horizon, about 95% say they expect to savor that time, and only 5% worry that they might be lonely. That's quite the contrast with popular stereotypes of single people, which insists that most single people are lonely and that getting married will cure that. Neither is true.

# 27

# What Do Many of the Most Influential Philosophers in History Have in Common?

A professor of philosophy looked into the lives of the <u>most influential philosophers</u> in history, and found that many of them had something in common. He sees their commonality as a problem that cries out for a solution.

Consider, first, many of the most celebrated male philosophers. Do you know what they have in common?

- Plato

- Augustine

- Aquinas

- Hobbes

- Locke

- Hume

- Adam Smith

- Descartes

- Spinoza

- Leibniz

- Kant

- Bentham

- Schopenhauer

- Kierkegaard

- Nietzche

- Sartre

- Wittgenstein

If you guessed that they are were all lifelong single people, you are correct! Most of them also had no children.

Now consider some of the most influential female philosophers:

- Simone de Beauvoir

- Hannah Arendt

- Simone Weil

- Iris Murdoch

Jonathan Wolff, the philosophy professor and author of the essay in question, notes that none of these women had children. (He didn't discuss their marital status.)

I'm not a philosopher, so I don't know how this list compares to the bigger list of all of the most influential philosophers. But it sure seems likely that the rate of lifelong singlehood (and maybe of not having children) is far greater among famous philosophers than it is among the general population.

What do you make of all this? Think about it for a moment, before reading on.

Wolff titles his essay, "Why do philosophers make unsuitable life partners?" He offers three possible answers, other than coincidence:

1. "the sheer oddity of philosophers makes them unsuitable life partners"

2. "domestic bliss dulls the philosophical edge"

3. "If genius is 'the infinite capacity for taking pains,' it wouldn't seem to leave much time for anything else."

He thinks that ordinary philosophers do not need to work so much that they have little time for anything else. In fact, he thinks that among his colleagues, those with children do better at "work-life balance" than those who do not have kids. "If you are looking after your children," Wolff suggests, "it puts your academic work into perspective. Maybe it isn't the most important thing in the world after all."

He has a solution for the problem of the academic philosopher who works too hard: "We need to make [academic] advancement dependent on what academics do during normal working hours, rather than their evenings and weekends."

I see things differently.

First, who says philosophers "make unsuitable life partners" just because they stayed single? Maybe they would have done just fine as life partners if that's what they wanted, but it wasn't. Maybe they *chose* to live single.

Maybe influential philosophers are not odd in some weirdo way that Wolff is suggesting. Maybe they are free thinkers who are unconventional in ways that helped make them the brilliant thinkers they are. Maybe free thinkers are unlikely to be attracted to conventional marriage or family life.

Maybe the famous philosophers did not stay single because their work took up so much of their time, and if only it had taken up less, they would have married. Maybe they loved their life of the mind. Maybe they wanted to be absorbed by their work. Or maybe, even if they did not spend all their time on their work, they still would not have been drawn to marriage or parenting. These philosophers are, by some criteria, extraordinary people. Maybe they were uninterested in living ordinary lives.

In short, unlike Wolff, I do not see commitment to the life of the mind as a problem that needs to be solved. I think it is something to be applauded.

I also don't like Wolff's belief that people with children (and I think he means, specifically, people who are married with children) are better than everyone else because they have the "perspective" that is supposedly lacking among some of the most brilliant minds of all time.

And as for his solution? I think he wants a 40-hour work week but he does not want to be disadvantaged in his career relative to those who work more hours – perhaps by choice. So would all philosophers be barred from working as many hours as they like? Would only the first 40 hours of their work count toward their tenure and promotion? How would that be monitored? How would it be enforced?

Wolff says that his goal is to wipe out "indirect discrimination" against parents by creating "a new model of academic progression that is fair to everyone." But how would his model be fair to people who love their work and are totally devoted to it? Maybe they are the people whose work will have an impact on many other people's lives for generations to come.

# 28

# Why So Many Romantic Partners Want to Be Both Together and Single

An essay by Isabelle Tessier, "I want to be single – but with you," zipped around the internet, rapidly amassing Likes and shares.

Here are some examples of what Tessier means when she fantasizes about the man to whom she would say, "I want to live a single life with you":

*"I want to eat with you, want you to make me talk about me and for you to talk about you... I want to imagine the loft of our dreams, knowing that we will probably never move in together.*

*"I don't always want to be invited for your evenings out and I don't always want to invite you to mine.*

*"I want to be your good friend, the one with whom you love hanging out. I want you to keep your desire to flirt with other girls, but for you to come back to me to finish your evening. Because I will want to go home with you. I want to be the one with whom you love to make love and fall asleep...For our couple life, would be the equivalent of our single lives today, but together."*

What Tessier does *not* want is what is celebrated in so many love songs – the longing among couples to be each other's everything. In *Singled Out*, I called that "intensive coupling" and described it this way:

*"Serious partners, in our current cultural fantasy, are the twosomes who look to each other for companionship, intimacy, caring, friendship, advice, the sharing of the tasks and finances of household and family, and just about everything else. They are the repositories for each other's hopes and dreams. They are each other's soul mates and sole mates. They are Sex and Everything Else Partners."*

Tessier does not want to be enmeshed with the partner she fantasizes about having. There are hints that many other couples are moving away from the model of intensive coupling, too. For example, in *Alone Together*, Paul Amato and his colleagues reported that couples in 2000, compared to couples in 1980, were less likely to go out together for fun, have their main meal together, work around the house together, or have as many friends in common.

Also relevant is the practice known as "living apart together." These "dual dwelling duos" are couples who choose to live apart from each other, and not because they have to for some reason (such as having jobs in different places) or because they want to feel free to cheat on each other without getting caught or because they are not really sure they want to be together. They simply want a place of their own, and they want their relationship, too. Many are married and some are even married with children. I devoted an entire chapter to them in *How We Live Now: Redefining Home and Family in the 21st Century*. They illustrate the contemporary cravings for both time alone as well as time together.

What I find intriguing about Tessier's essay is her framing of the live she covets. She calls it single life, even though what she is describing sure sounds a lot like some version of coupled life. The title of her article is, "I want to be single – but with you." It isn't, "I want to be some kind of couple, just not the 'you-are-my-everything' kind."

After decades in which living single has been stereotyped and stigmatized, is it now becoming something that even couples want a piece of?

Another striking example came from Kate Bolick's *Spinster: Making a Life of One's Own*. Her goal, Bolick said, was not "a wholesale reclamation of the word *spinster*..." Instead, she wanted to offer the word "as a shorthand for holding on to that in you which is independent and self-sufficient, whether you're single or coupled." Again, coupled people get to call themselves single, too.

Is this really happening? Are couples really trying to say, "Hey, I'm single, too!" If so, I think I like it.

# 29

# Why Would Committed Couples Live Apart If They Don't Have to?

In 2006, more than half of the participants in a British Social Attitudes Survey agreed with the statement that members of a couple "do not need to live together to have a strong relationship." Nearly two-thirds agreed that "relationships are much stronger when both partners have the independence to follow their own careers and friendships."

Among couples – including committed and even married couples – a nontrivial percentage are "living apart together." These dual-dwelling duos include many who are in the relationship for the long haul, but they are not in the same home. The article reporting the results of the British survey (reference is at the end) estimates that 10 percent of British adults live apart from a partner.

For quite some time, we have been familiar with "commuter marriages" maintained by couples who have to live apart because of job requirements. Those arrangements strike me as a lot less interesting than the more voluntary ones – the couples living in separate homes not because they have to but because they want to.

But why would couples choose to live apart when living together is more expected, more romanticized, and more affordable?

In the British survey, respondents were offered only four reasons to endorse as to why they chose to live apart: "I prefer not to live with my partner," "My partner prefers not to live with me," "We just don't want to live together" and "We both want to keep our homes." Nearly half of the survey participants chose at least one of those answers. (Those who said they were living apart because they had little choice in the matter described constraints such as job locations, university locations, or responsibilities for caring for an elderly relative.)

Referring to reasons offered by participants in other studies of committed couples living apart, the authors noted that by maintaining homes of their own,

*"...they can experience both the intimacy and satisfaction of being in a couple, and at the same time better continue with important pre-existing commitments and identities that living together might otherwise preclude, such as caring for children or dependent parents, maintaining personal social networks, keeping cherished houses or possessions, or simply avoiding the problems they feel might result from living together."*

I think these are all intriguing reasons, but did you notice what is missing from the list?

It is the desire or need for solitude. I wonder how many coupled people live apart not because they cherish their home only as a possession, but also as a place where they have their own time and their own space. In survey research in which participants simply agree or disagree with the statements that are presented to them, there is no opportunity to learn about motivations that are not included in the list of statements.

**Reference:** Duncan, S., & Phillips, M. (2010). People who live apart together (LATs) – how different are they? *The Sociological Review, 58,* 112-134.

# 30

# Quiet Time:
# Do We Need It Now More Than Ever?

Are there any truly quiet places left, free of the din of all of the noises made by humans? There are so many more unnatural noises than there ever were before. We have all our beeping, buzzing, nudging devices. We have stuff that hums that we don't even notice, such as our refrigerators. Many of us are within earshot of traffic even when we are at home. A population that just keeps growing, spreading into previously pristine spaces, also adds to the noise.

For his book with John Grossmann, _One Square Inch of Silence_, Gordon Hempton traveled the country in search of untouched places and recording what he heard there. Hempton considers himself an "acoustic ecologist." (I had never heard of such a thing.) In *One Square Inch*, he and Grossmann make this case for the significance of silence:

> "Good things come from a quiet place. Study, prayer, music, transformation, worship, communion. The words peace and quiet are all but synonymous, often spoken in the same breath. A quiet place is the think tank of the soul – the spawning ground of truth and beauty.

> "A quiet place outdoors has no physical borders or limits to perception. One can commonly hear for miles and listen even farther. A quiet place affords sanctuary for the soul, where the difference between right and wrong becomes more readily apparent. It is a place to feel the love that connects all things, large and small, human and not; a place where the presence of a tree can be heard. A quiet place is a place to open up all your senses and come alive."

In "Personal Havens," a story Grossmann wrote for the Winter 2009 edition of *Creative Living* magazine, the author makes the case that our need for private havens, where we can find some quiet, is greater than it has ever been before.

But is it really? Or have we grown so accustomed to being tethered to our cell phones and other gadgets, so accustomed to having our favorite music and TV shows and movies on demand, that we don't even want silence anymore? Are we becoming allergic to sitting alone with our own thoughts?

I don't know of any research on whether people want or need more quiet time than they did before. The book titled *Quiet* was a big-time bestseller, so maybe that's indicative of something, though the topic was more about introverts than about quiet.

Personally, I've become more comfortable with sounds in contexts where I never wanted them before. I grew up with two brothers and a sister, and a father who liked having the TV on all the time. (My mother didn't make much noise.) Sometimes, the only way I could do my reading or homework was to go into my parents' closet, turn on the light, and close the door. The clothes would muffle all the sounds, and I could work in peace.

Now I'd be claustrophobic before the first minute had passed. And now that I live alone, there is no need to hide out. I have my whole place to myself. But here's the thing: Sometimes I turn on music while I'm writing. And if what I'm writing takes up little of my mental space (for example, emailing), I can even do some of that with the TV on.

I still crave utter silence, though, or just the kinds of sounds you hear in nature. I go out for walks almost every day – there are so many great trails here in Santa Barbara – but I never listen to music when I do.

So, do we need more quiet than we ever did before? Or have most of us accommodated to all the human-made noises to such an extent that we actually want them in our lives more than we ever did before? As social scientists like to say, more research is needed.

# 31

# A First for Humans?
# People Now Eat Alone More Often Than with Others

What could be more sociable than the act of sharing a meal or a drink?

For years, I've been researching and writing about one particular variety of eating alone – dining alone in restaurants. I have found that people are often very self-conscious about dining solo. They think other people are thinking mean and dismissive things about them when they do. Those fears, it turns out, are overblown. Other people are just as likely to be catty about the couple they see at the next table.

In my research and casual conversations, there are always people who say that they refrain from dining on their own but not because they are worried about what other people would think of them. Instead, they say that they just don't want to. Meals are supposed to be sociable events, they say. It's boring to go out to dinner by yourself.

And yet, a new report of Americans' 2013 eating and drinking habits across all venues (not just dining out) comes to a stunning conclusion: When we are eating or drinking, well over half the time, we are doing that alone.

Here are the specifics:

- **60** percent of the time, people eat **breakfast** by themselves

- **55** percent of the time, people eat **lunch** by themselves

- **32** percent of the time, people eat **dinner** by themselves

- **More than 70** percent of the time, people eat **between meals** by themselves

- Across all the different times when people are eating or drinking, **nearly 60** percent of them occur when people are alone.

[An important caveat: The market research group who put out the report, NPD group, offered just a two-page summary. I don't know the details of how the study was conducted.]

I don't know if 2013 marked the first year that the act of eating became a predominantly solitary activity. Maybe that first happened a year or several years ago. In the big sweep of history, though, I bet it is something truly new and unique.

The report offered no hints as to why this is happening, but it is easy to generate possibilities. Perhaps most importantly, the number of single people, and the number of people who live alone, has been growing for decades.

But with such high rates of eating alone, it can't be just single people or solo-dwellers who are driving the trends. In research that is at least indirectly relevant, marriage researchers have found that in 2000, married couples were less likely to eat together than they were in 1980.

Growing time pressures are a likely culprit. Meals with other people are probably, on the average, more leisurely than meals enjoyed alone (though they surely do not have to be). Anecdotally, solo diners seem to be served more quickly than people dining with others.

Perhaps also relevant is how easy it is to entertain ourselves when we are on our own. Personally, I don't mind daydreaming or thinking through something I've been trying to figure out while I'm eating. But for those who prefer external distractions, our gadgets make those oh so easy to access.

# 32

# How Many People Say It Is Important to Have Times When They Are Completely Alone?

How important is it to you to have times when you are completely alone, away from anyone else?

The Pew Research Center asked a representative sample of American adults that question. Their options were:

- very important

- somewhat important

- not very important

- not at all important

- don't know

Results showed that Americans really like their alone time. More than half (55%) said it was very important to be able to have time completely alone, away from everyone else, and another 30% said it was somewhat important, for a grand total of 85% saying it was important to have time to spend completely alone. (In the minority were the 9% who said it was not very important and the 2% who said it was not at all important. Another 2% said they didn't know. The other 2% didn't answer.)

Participants were also asked about the significance of their homes as places where they are not disturbed. Results were nearly identical. A total of 85% said it was important that they not be disturbed at home (56% very important and 29% somewhat important, as compared to just 9% who said it was not very important and 2% who said it was not at all important).

In the research I did for my book, <u>*How We Live Now: Redefining Home and Family in the 21st Century*</u>, I traveled the country, asking people to show me their homes and tell me about their lives. I went into the project expecting everyone to want at least some time alone and some time with other people, though in vastly different proportions.

Occasionally, I met a person who claimed to have little or no interest in having time to themselves. But as we continued to talk, there almost always came a time when they waxed poetic about a particular time of the day when they were totally on their own and just loved it. Typically, it was an early morning hour, when no one else was up.

So, are there really people for whom it is "not at all important" to have time to be completely alone? Are there people who really do get no time at all that is all to themselves – and like it that way? I suppose there are a few but my guess is that their numbers are dwindling.

# Alone in Public: Dining Alone, Traveling Alone, Alone in a Crowd

# More Americans Are Dining Alone and Traveling Alone. Here's Why.

When I taught a psychology course on singles in America at the University of Virginia in 1999, one of the assignments was: Go out to dinner alone. One of my students waited patiently as the hostess seated one party after another; the hostess thought my student was waiting for someone else, so she ignored her. Another student got dressed up and headed to an upscale restaurant with several dining rooms. She was ushered into a room with no other diners.

Today, things would be different. Recently, the online restaurant reservation service Open Table reported that, over the past two years, the fastest-growing party size has been tables for one; one-person reservations have increased 62 percent. Diners are not going to restaurants alone just by chance — they are committing to it ahead of time.

Solo travel has also increased. In a 2015 survey from Visa, 24 percent said that the last time they traveled overseas for fun, they went alone. Two years before, that number was just 15 percent. When respondents to another survey were asked whether they would take a vacation on their own if they had the opportunity, 40 percent said yes.

A confluence of changes in demographics, business practices and technology have contributed to the embrace of solo experiences. But the most significant is the rise of people who live alone — now about one in seven adults.

If more Americans are used to living alone, going out alone is no longer such an aberration. In 1999, when my students were being ignored and ushered into empty dining rooms, 26.6 million people in the United States lived alone. Now it is nearly 35 million.

If you were to travel around the country knocking on doors at random, you would more often find a person living alone than a family of a mom, dad and kids. Having a place of your own is more likely to convey cachet than loneliness. Many young people believe that when they can afford to live alone for the first time, they have officially crossed the threshold into adulthood. For older people, having the financial wherewithal to live alone is their ticket to a more dignified and joyful life than being in an institution. So appealing is a place of one's own that a substantial number of committed couples – including even married ones – are living apart because they like it that way.

Over the past half a century or so, even children have gotten a taste of what it's like to have their own space. Rather than sharing a room with siblings, kids whose parents can afford it have their own rooms. And it is not just in the "Home Alone" movies that kids have the whole place to themselves. As more mothers entered the workforce, and as the number of single-parent households increased, the ranks of latchkey kids really started to grow. By 1998, more than 8 million children between the ages of 5 and 14 were spending time on their own with no adults around.

The kids let themselves into their empty homes, do their homework, entertain themselves and prepare their own snacks – good practice for living alone later on. Many of these children grew fond of their autonomy and their space. Living with a roommate was once the iconic college experience; now universities are inundated with requests for private rooms. At Montclair State University, for example, about 15 percent of freshmen living on campus have private rooms. Harvard University has been renovating its residential houses, with an emphasis on increasing the number of single rooms. And at the University of Pennsylvania, just about every student who requests a private room can get one.

The rise in the number of people living alone adds to the number of people potentially interested in dining alone or traveling alone: Solo dwellers get practice being alone privately before doing it publicly.

But savoring your solitude in a place of your own, outside of the public gaze, is different from venturing out where everyone can see you. Business owners have noticed the rise of solo customers, and are now catering to them — creating the kinds of venues and experiences those customers crave. For example, at the Founding Farmers restaurants in the Washington area, solo diners are sometimes offered free cocktails and appetizers. Hosts are trained to be sensitive to whether these guests might want to chat. Some restaurants offer tables for one in prime locations (no more being hidden in the back, next to the swinging kitchen doors), as well as alternatives such as bar seating or communal tables.

Back when I was teaching that class on singles, I would ask students if they ever went out to dinner alone, and if not, why. Some insisted that they weren't deterred by self-consciousness but by the more mundane concern that they'd be bored. Well, that's no longer the case.

Our ubiquitous devices offer endless entertainment and constant virtual companionship. We can browse websites, play Candy Crush, read books, text or tweet at our friends. Then, once our food arrives, instead of downing it as fast as possible and dashing out the door, we pause, take a picture and post it on Instagram for all the world to see.

It's easier to be alone because we never really are.

[This was originally published in the *Washington Post*.]

# 34

# The Psychology of Being Alone in Public

When I taught the graduate course, "Singles in society," years ago, one of the assignments was for students to go out for a meal by themselves. The students were totally into it. They upped the ante: It had to be dinner, not lunch. And then they upped it again: They could not bring anything to distract them during dinner, such as something to read or to look at. They had to just dine on their own.

One undergraduate persuaded me to let her into this graduate class, and when she told her friends about the assignment, they were horrified. They could not imagine going out to dinner by themselves.

The graduate students, and the aghast friends of the undergraduates, were all onto something. Their intuitions have been supported by a series of studies reported by a pair of marketing researchers.

## Going Out Alone, Just for Fun? No, Thank You

People are reluctant to do things, just for fun, in public by themselves. Asked about the possibility of going out to dinner or going to a movie in a theater, they express more interest in the experience, and expect to enjoy it more, if they are going to go with friends than if they are going to be alone.

Their reluctance can be explained, at least in part, by how they think they will be viewed by other people. If they are out in restaurants or movie theaters by themselves, they think others will look at them and assume they don't have many friends. That's probably why my undergraduate's friends were horrified at the thought of going out to dinner alone – they thought other people would see them as losers.

The researchers found that the reluctance to go to a movie theater alone (compared to going with friends) and the expectation of being judged harshly for doing so, was not just true of people in the U.S. People in India and China shared the same psychology of being alone in public.

## Out Alone for a Purpose (Not Just for Fun)? That Sounds Better

My students who insisted on taking the assignment to the next level, by prohibiting themselves from bringing reading materials or any other semblance of work, were correct in their intuitions that going out in public just to enjoy yourself would be more difficult. For example, in one of the studies, participants imagined being in a coffee shop just having a drink, or they imagined doing some work while they were there. And, as usual, they imagined doing those things either on their own or with friends.

If they were going to be alone in the coffee shop, they preferred to be working. They thought they would enjoy the experience more when they were working than when they were just sipping their drink. They also thought others would judge them more harshly (as a person who has few friends) when they were just sipping than when they were sipping and working.

The psychology flipped when they imagined being at the coffee shop with friends. They thought they'd enjoy it more if they were all just hanging out than if they were working. They expected to be viewed more positively by others, too, if they were just hanging out than if they were working.

The concern with what others might be thinking seemed to be paramount. In another one of the studies, participants were asked to imagine that they were going out to a movie either by themselves or with friends. Did they prefer to see the movie on a Saturday night or a Sunday? At a time when the theater was full or when it was not so full?

You can probably guess the results. Participants would prefer to go to the theater on a Sunday night, and to a less crowded theater, if they were going to be on their own. They preferred Saturday night, and a full theater, if they were with friends. The people who were going to the movie alone did not want to be seen, and they figured there was a better chance of escaping the notice of other people on a Sunday night when the theater was less crowded.

One of the interesting things about these studies is that they show that people are not always reluctant to be alone in public. In the coffee shop study, for example, when people had the cover of doing work, they were not so hesitant to be there on their own. Another study showed that when people were out in public for some practical reason, such as getting groceries or getting some exercise, they actually preferred being on their own than with friends.

## Home Alone Watching Movies or Playing Video Games? Now That's Just Fine

Readers of this blog probably already know that people who are single at heart savor their time alone; they don't dread it. The research on the psychology of being alone found that even for people more generally (not just those who are single-at-heart), there are experiences they look forward to enjoying by themselves. For example, people are generally more interested in watching movies at home, or playing video games on their computers, by themselves than with their friends. They think they'd enjoy those experiences more that way.

## But Wait – How Do People *Actually* Feel When Alone in Public?

In all the studies I've described so far, people were asked to imagine how they would feel in various situations. That's important, because if you think about going out to dinner or a movie by yourself, and you get a bad feeling about it, you might not go. But what if you did end up going? How would you feel then?

In the key study, participants were recruited from the student union to visit the university art gallery. Students who were by themselves at the student union went to the gallery by themselves and students who were with a friend went to the gallery with their friend. (That's not ideal, methodologically; random assignment would have been better.) The art gallery had glass walls, so other people could easily see the students as they looked at the exhibit.

Before they left the student union for the art gallery, the participants were asked to predict how they would feel. As in the other studies, the students who were headed to the gallery on their own thought that they would enjoy it less than the students who were going there with a friend. They also expressed less interest in attending similar exhibits. Also consistent with the other studies in which participants only imagined what their experience would be like, the people who were going to the gallery alone, more so than those going with a friend, thought that other people would judge them harshly.

After the participants spent time in the art gallery, they were asked the same questions again. Now, there were hardly any differences! The students who spent time at the art gallery on their own enjoyed it every bit as much as the students who went there with a friend. They were equally interested in seeing similar exhibits in the future. And the difference between the students who were alone and those who were with a friend, in their guesses about how other people judged them, was smaller than it was before.

The moral of this research is that we probably worry too much about doing things alone. We think we won't enjoy the experience, but we may well enjoy it just as much as we would with friends.

That concern that we have about other people judging us harshly if they see us alone doing fun things in public? That's probably unwarranted. One of the very first studies I ever did that was relevant to single life was about how people in restaurants are judged by others, depending on whether they are alone or with others. My colleagues and I conducted a very elaborate study, in which we photographed different sets of people sitting at a booth in a restaurant. There were always two men and two women. Then we photoshopped the photos, so that each person sometimes appeared to be dining alone, sometimes with a person of the other gender, sometimes with a person of the same gender, sometimes with two of the three other people, and sometimes with everyone (likely seen as two couples).

Then we recruited lots of people to look at the photos and tell us what they thought. We expected them to judge the people dining alone most harshly. We were surprised – but also happy – to find that we were wrong. People sometimes did say dismissive and unkind things about the solo diners, but they were just as likely to say dismissive and unkind things about the exact same people pictured with one other person (as if they were there as a couple) or more than one person. Sometimes the judges said nice things. That, too, was just as likely to happen when the person in the photo appeared to be dining alone as when the same person was pictured with another person or persons.

Next time you are considering doing something on your own but you are feeling hesitant, know that research has a suggestion for you: Try it. You will probably like it.

**Reference**: Ratner, R. K., & Hamilton, R. W. (2015). Inhibited from bowling alone. *Journal of Consumer Research, 42*, 266-283.

# 35

## Has Dining Solo Lost Its Stigma?

How do you feel about walking into a restaurant on your own? I don't mean just a fast food restaurant, but a real, sit-down-and-take-your-time sort of place. If your answer is not entirely positive, how do you explain your negative feelings? Are you worried about what other people might think of you if they see you eating alone?

When I first started doing research on single life more than a decade ago, one of the first sets of studies I conducted with my colleagues was designed to address the question: What do other people really think of you when you dine alone?

The research was very careful and systematic. It was never published, though, because all of my predictions turned out to be wrong. The ways that solo diners are judged turned out to differ hardly at all from how couples or pairs of friends or groups of three people are viewed.

In the study, we took pictures of sets of four people – two men and two women each time – as they ate dinner in a restaurant. Some of the sets of people were young adults, and others were middle aged.

We used photoshop to airbrush out one or more of the people at the table. So, some pictures included the original four people, others included just two people (sometimes a man and a woman; sometimes two men; sometimes two women); others included three people; and the key pictures included just one person dining solo.

What was important about the technique of photoshopping is that each diner had the exact same facial expression and posture in each version of the photo. That way, if other people judged the solo diners more harshly (which is what we expected), it wouldn't be because the solo diners actually appeared more despondent than the coupled diners did.

We showed the pictures to hundreds of other people, and asked them to rate the diners in the pictures. We also asked them to offer their own thoughts as to why the person was dining alone (in the solo diner picture) or with the other person(s) in the other pictures.

People looking at the photos of the solo diners did sometimes offer just the sorts of harsh judgments we anticipated. For example, they said things like, "Doesn't have any friends;" "He is lonely;" and "She looks depressed."

More interesting were all of the positive and nonjudgmental assessments that were offered. For example:

- "Wanted to relax."

- "Traveling."

- "He seems to be enjoying his dinner."

- "Enjoying a few peaceful moments."

- "She just wanted to eat by herself."

- "Wanted time to ponder."

- "He is secure."

When we coded the comments that were made about the male-female pairs and compared them statistically to the comments about the solo diners, we found the same mix of both positive and negative comments, and in the same proportions.

Examples of positive comments made about the couples were that they were having a "fine, quiet conversation;" that "they enjoy spending time together;" or that "they are very close."

The more negative comments about the couples included:

- "He thought he liked her."

- "She is upset."

- They went to dinner "to have a talk because their relationship needs some mending."

- She went to dinner with him "out of obligation – she's married to him."

No matter what we did to try to compare the solo diners to everyone else (not just the male-female pairs but the other pairs and groupings, too), we just could not find any way in which the solo diners were viewed more harshly than any other sets of diners.

Have you seen the 1984 movie, *The Lonely Guy*? In a key scene, Steve Martin walks into a restaurant on his own, and a spotlight suddenly appears and follows him to his table. So do the eyes of all of the other diners, who become speechless as they watch the spectacle. A comic exaggeration, sure, but it seemed to resonate with many people who dare not dine alone.

I wonder, though, whether that feeling of dread is changing. Are more people dining solo? I don't know that, but it would be interesting to find out. A recent story in the *Washington Post* noted that diners often bring their digital devices with them, almost treating them as companions. Do those devices make it easier for people to dine solo without feeling self-conscious? That was suggested by one of the people the reporter interviewed.

The observation I most appreciated was offered by Sherry Turkle, a leading scholar of the place of technology in our lives. She gave a thumbs-down to digital fiddling while dining out, saying, "Having a solitary meal in a restaurant is a basic spiritual practice. It's classic way to experience moments of solitude and to refresh and restore and gather yourself."

Maybe that will become the 21st century sense of solo dining.

# 36

# What's So Great About Traveling on Your Own

When Abigail Butcher was in her twenties, the mere thought of traveling on her own made her "recoil with dread." She had the usual fears that people harbor about traveling alone or even dining alone – that other people will think you are a loser with no friends, or you might find the experience boring, or you might miss out on all the fun you would have if you were doing those things with other people.

Now she is 38 and single, and a freelance journalist in the UK with the travel beat as one of her specialties. She's tried many variations of traveling with others – with groups, with a close friend, with a romantic partner – and she's also done plenty of traveling on her own. It is solo travel that she recommends most enthusiastically. Now, even when she is in a relationship, she usually chooses to travel on her own.

In one of her articles, she explains what makes solo travel so appealing to her:

- "When I venture abroad solo, I connect with my surroundings, the people I meet and the thoughts in my own head on a much deeper level."

- "I use travel to reassess life, contemplate my future and treat myself to some down time."

- She doesn't always want to engage in long conversations when she's traveling on her own and she doesn't have to: "I'll happily talk to anyone but only on my terms."

- She loves "eating meals alone with a book and a glass of local wine."

- "I've made wonderful, lifelong friendships on my trips with people I may not even have met had I not been alone."

- After returning home from her solo travels, she feels "more grounded, energetic and more ready to tackle the world."

After reading her story on traveling solo, I was curious about her and found her website. A fun fact I learned about her: she was once the news editor of a magazine called *Horse and Hound*. (Who thought up a magazine on horses and hounds?) Considering her sensibility about solo travel, I wasn't surprised that she had this to say about her life: "I am hugely fortunate to love my job, and combine my passions in life with what I do for a living."

That's what successful single people do – they find meaningful work, pursue their passions, and live their lives fully, joyfully, and unapologetically.

# 37

# What Do You Really Know About the Experience of Traveling Solo?

More than a decade ago, when I first started to study single life in earnest and not just live it, I took a look at how different groups and markets seemed to view single people. One of them was the travel industry, and wow, was I appalled. I found appeals written for the single traveler, but they all seemed to assume that people traveling on their own had just one goal – to come home coupled. Marketers touted all the eligible suitors the solo travelers might meet and all the wonderful social events on the schedule to bring them together. And if singles were charged far more for their reservations than couples, well too bad.

Today, much has changed for the better. There is no better chronicler of solo sojourners and their place in the contemporary travel industry than *New York Times* writer Stephanie Rosenbloom (also mentioned in previous posts here and here and here). In "Travel Industry Responds to Rise in Solo Sojourners," I found 5 fun facts that either surprised or delighted me. I'm presenting them in the form of quiz items. See how many you can get correct:

1. Think about people who travel for fun, and not in their own country. Of all those people around the globe pursuing leisure travel in different lands, what percentage of them do you think are traveling on their own?

2. Who do you think is doing the vast majority of that solo traveling, the stereotypically brave, rugged individualist men or the women who are stereotypically the cowering fragile flowers fearing for their safety?

3. Of those Americans who are 45 and older and have traveled solo, do you think more of them are married or unmarried (either single or divorced)?

4. What's your guess about how solo travelers react to experiences? Specifically, for the 45 and older group (I'm talking about them

because AARP has made survey data available for that group), what percentage of solo sojourners liked it enough to plan to travel alone again in the next 12 months?

5. As more and more people make it clear that they are interested in traveling on their own, how has the travel industry responded?

      a. They know they can soak this eager, expanding customer base, so solo travel is becoming even more expensive.

      b. More companies are offering more deals and better deals for the solo sojourners.

Now I'll put a bit of space between these questions and the answers by sharing a few choice quotes from the article.

- A woman who works for a travel agency with many baby boomers and seniors as customers explains why solo travel can be quite appealing to married mothers: "after having taken care of spouses and kids for so many years, it's nice to have an experience on one's own without worrying, 'Is Fred having a good time?'"

- As for what first-time solo travelers told Rosenbloom about what surprised them, one said, "Looking back, the one thing I wish I'd known was not to be so nervous the first time."

## ANSWERS:

1. 24 percent – nearly one in four

2. Solo travelers are overwhelmingly women

3. 53 percent are married (that surprised me)

4. More than 80 percent

5. b

# 38

# Alone in a Crowd:
# There's Something Special About It

Have you seen that cover of *New York Magazine* – the one with the pictures of the dozens of women who spoke out against Bill Cosby? It was so powerful that when I first saw it, it took my breath away. There was something else in that issue that I loved – a whole section, with lots of different brief and imaginative contributions by some wonderful writers, about spending time alone in New York City.

"Spending Time Alone: In a city that can provoke loneliness – but also reward solitude" opens with this:

> "In this crowded city of 8.4 million – in fact, the most crowded New York has ever been – one of the great and rare pleasures is finding solitude, whether on the subway or at the movies or in a booth facing the wall at a Chinatown noodle shop. But being alone when surrounded by so many others holds a different appeal from being alone in a cabin in the woods..."

Here are a few of my favorite quotes from the individual contributions:

On "Walking Alone," by Vivian Gornick:

> "Here, alone in the street, I feel free as I do nowhere else, except perhaps at my desk. There is no one to bore, embarrass, or threaten me. No one to whom I owe attention or from whom I need attention. I feel free to shop, dawdle, or move on as I will..."

On "Riding the Subway Alone," by Jennifer Szalai:

> "...That time on the train is mine. Nothing is expected of me...The time feels stolen, like something I didn't have before, though in truth it is the opposite: a drop of what was once in such steady supply that I didn't even notice it was there."

On "Seeing a Movie Alone," by Darin Strauss:

> "Maybe the romantic part derives from being alone. Alone is key. You know how Sinatra makes being dumped a decisive expression of the stylish adult? Alone is cool. Alone is how we start and what we return to."

On "Climbing the Empire State Building Alone," by Zach Woods:

> If you take the last elevator to the top at 1:15 a.m., "it's empty, it's beautiful, and the city sounds like the ocean."

On "Going to Coney Island Alone," by James Hannaham:

> "...it has become a solitary ritual. I always linger there, savoring the ocean air mixed with the scents of fried clams and asphalt, the eeriness of a nearly deserted carnival on a drab weekday, an atmosphere that practically impersonates memory."

On "Staying in a Hotel Alone," by Kate Bolick:

> "In this new life, I am my better self. Having someone else make the bed helps. I work industriously in the morning, run an errand at lunch. At dinner, I meet a friend. For two days, an unknown corner of the city is mine. I return home refreshsed."

On "Riding the Staten Island Ferry Alone," by Eileen Myles:

> "Being on the water is an animal thing, and that a great city continues to have a common and available appendage to its waters means New York remains cool, grotty, and plebian. Which is exactly this poet's studio or anyone's dream."

The special section also includes a sidebar on one of the most intriguing books on living alone: *Live Alone and Like It*, by Marjorie Hillis. I wrote about the book in "Advice to singles from an editor at *Vogue* – in 1936."

Not mentioned is another insightful and beautifully-written book, Anneli Rufus's *Party of One: The Loners' Manifesto*. I thought of Rufus in this context because she opens her book with a story of being alone in a crowd, "together with the crowd and yet apart." Then she begins her explanation of what loner really means, and it is not any of the scary things you have heard:

"Some of us *appear* to be in, but we are out. And that is where we want to be. Not just want but need...

"...an orientation, not just a choice. A fact...We are loners. Which means we are at our best, as Orsino says in *Twelfth Night*, when least in company."

# The Demographic Trend Sweeping the World: World:

# Living Alone

# 39

# Individualism Goes Global: More People Around the World Are Living Alone

For a long time, Western nations have been moving away from values that emphasize family ties and fitting in, and toward more individualistic values such as independence, uniqueness, personal choice, and self-expression. But does the same march toward individualism and away from collectivism also characterize other nations around the globe? That's the question Henri Santos, Michael Varnum, and Igor Grossman addressed in their 2017 article in *Psychological Science*, "Global increases in individualism."

The researchers were interested in individualistic *practices* (such as living alone) as well as individualistic *values* (such as valuing friends more than family, teaching children to be independent instead of obedient, and believing in freedom of speech). They found 51 years of data (1960 through 2011) from 78 countries. The countries were wide-ranging geographically, in their status as developed or developing nations, in their socioeconomic status, and much more. The social scientists' short answer to the question of whether individualism is on the rise world-wide is "yes."

Across all the countries in the study, individualistic practices and values increased about 12% between 1960 and 2011. Analyses of individualistic practices, such as living alone and divorcing, showed a substantial increase over time for 34 of the 41 countries with relevant data. Only four countries seemed headed away from individualism in their practices – Cameroon, Malawi, Malaysia, and Mali.

Analyses of individualistic values showed substantial increases over the five decades for 39 of the 53 nations with relevant data. Only five countries have been becoming notably less individualistic in their values – Armenia, China, Croatia, Ukraine, and Uruguay.

Professor Santos and his colleagues examined several factors that have been theorized as driving changes in individualism, such as socioeconomic development, frequency of disasters, presence of infectious diseases such as cholera and tuberculosis, and extremes in climate. By far, the most powerful factor was socioeconomic development. As education, income, and the proportion of white collar (compared to blue collar) jobs increased, so, too, did individualistic practices and values in subsequent years. As the authors noted, "most of the countries that did not show an increase in individualistic values were among the lowest in socioeconomic development." China was an exception.

The global rise in living alone had already been documented and discussed in detail in Eric Klinenberg's *Going Solo* and Lynn Jamieson and Roona Simpson's *Living Alone*. What is striking and new in the 78-nation study is the range of practices and values that were examined (see the section below on the details of the study), the statistical documentation of the increase of individualism over five decades, and the examination of the factors linked to the increase. The finding of a trend toward valuing friends over family is especially noteworthy, at a time when traditional ties such as marriage and family continue to be extravagantly celebrated and rewarded, even in some of the wealthiest nations.

## What Are the Implications of the Rise of Individualism and Decline of Collectivism?

Is the rise of individualism something we should applaud or fear? *How We Live Now: Redefining Home and Family in the 21st Century* offers some perspective:

*The rise of individualism has, for many, been exhilarating. People who never did feel comfortable with marrying or parenting or living in the suburbs or handing over their lifelong loyalty to a single employer, for instance, are liberated from soul-crushing strictures and expectations. People who once believed that no one in the world shared their quirks or maladies discover others like them everywhere and can share their lives online and off. Individuals of all stripes can design their own lives, filling them with the people and places and spaces and pursuits that they find most engaging, most authentic, and most meaningful.*

*For others, though, the new developments are ominous and even terrifying. People who prefer certainty, predictability, and commitments that are bolted in place by powerful institutions and revered traditions feel insecure and adrift in the brave new world of individualism…*

*The trade-off between the security of a set path through life with a small, dense set of enduring relationships and the freedom of an ever-growing cache of opportunities is one for the ages. It is not a unique dilemma of modern life. What is often lost in the debates is that opportunities are not obligations. I met people, young and old, without televisions or Facebook accounts. And just because you can live alone far away from the place where you were born does not mean that you can no longer choose to live with family and across the street from lifelong friends in the town where you grew up.*

## Details of the 78-Nation Study

Four individualistic **practices** were examined:

1. *Living alone*: The percentage of households with only one member.

2. *Living alone among adults 60 and older*: Important in showing that older people are more often living alone rather than with family.

3. *Household size*: In individualistic societies, households are smaller.

4. *Divorce*: The ratio of divorced and separated people to married and widowed people. Divorce is more characteristic of individualistic societies.

Three individualistic **values** were assessed:

1. *Valuing friends more than family.* Participants rated the importance of their friends and the importance of their family; the ratings were compared. Valuing friends more than family is a way of valuing individualism over collectivism.

2. *Teaching children to be independent.* Participants indicated whether it was important to teach the value of independence – an individualistic value – to their children. Collectivist values emphasize obedience instead.

3. *Valuing political self-expression.* Participants were asked to choose among four goals for their country. Their values were categorized as individualistic if they chose at least one of the two goals describing self-expression: "Protecting freedom of speech" and "Giving people more say in important government decisions."

The authors averaged over the four practices to come up with one measure of individualistic practices. They also averaged over the three values to create one measure of individualistic values. Separate analyses of the individual practices and values were not reported.

*The 78 nations*: The first dozen names on the alphabetical list of the 78 nations offer a sense of the range of countries included in the research: Albania, Argentina, Armenia, Austria, Australia, Azerbaijan, Bangladesh, Bolivia, Brazil, Burkina Faso, Canada, and Cameroon.

# The Many Different Ways of Living Alone

When you think about people living alone, do you imagine them in a house in an isolated location, with no one else nearby? Or do you visualize them in an apartment of their own, in a building with lots of people all around them, only they don't know any of them? Those are some of the kinds of living arrangements that count as living alone, but there are others, too.

I live in a house by myself. I moved to my neighborhood knowing no one else around me. Of course, by now I've met some other people in this tiny town of Summerland, California, but I didn't move here because I knew other people who lived here too.

In college, I lived alone at the other extreme. For several years, I had a single room in a dorm. There was a sense in which I was living alone. As soon as I walked out my door, though, I had other people all around me up and down the hallway and above and beneath me on the other floors. We all shared the same dining room. I liked that a lot at the time. Now, it would be far too much togetherness.

For my book, _How We Live Now: Redefining Home and Family in the 21st Century_, I interviewed people about their living arrangements and found that some adults are recreating those kinds of living situations for themselves. In one example of shared housing, people all live in the same house, but each person (or set of people) has private space. You can walk into your space – it may be one room or a whole suite – and shut the door behind you. You have your privacy and your solitude. Open your door, though, and you may run into your housemates in the hallways or in the spaces you share, such as a living room or dining room.

The people I met who were sharing a home had different preferences for the amount of social interaction they wanted with their housemates. Some had regularly scheduled times to get together – often for a meal – as well as more informal gatherings, such as a spontaneously declared movie night. Another person I interviewed, whose housemates include family, said that he and his sibling often do little more than grunt at one another as they pass in the hallways – and that's just fine.

People who live in different parts of a duplex, or on different floors of a multi-story home, have even more privacy, but they are less alone than I am now. (Again, I'm talking about geographical aloneness rather than emotional loneliness – very different! I savor my own space but I would not want to feel emotionally alone.)

One of my friends from Virginia who lived alone for a long time described a living arrangement that she loved. She had her own place, but several close friends lived within walking distance. They often sauntered to each other's places then headed out for dinner. That's a different kind of "alone" than the kind that requires some sort of transportation to get to your nearest friend.

Discussions about living alone are usually discussions of people who are single, and that is appropriate. There are some intriguing exceptions, though. For example, there are committed couples – including married couples, and even married couples with children – who are living in their own separate homes because that's how they want to live. The practice even has its own name: "living apart together."

A *New York Times* story described a married couple in which each person lives in a separate little bungalow on the same lot. For the woman, it was her condition for marrying – she would only do it if she could have her own place. For other couples, even that arrangement would mean too much proximity.

Many adults in the U.S. and beyond are struggling to create a life with just the right mix of time alone and time together. It is a luxurious struggle to have. We don't all have to live the same way anymore.

# Living Alone: 11 Things You Didn't Know

Think you know what it means to live alone? Even if you are have your own personal experiences living solo, and know lots of other people who do, too, chances are that you have been misled by the media and other myth-makers about what solo life is really like.

The most significant, intensive, and far-reaching study of solo living is described in Eric Klinenberg's 2012 book, _Going Solo: The Extraordinary Rise and Surprising Appeal of Living Alone_. Here are 11 of the many revelations about solo living that you can find in the book.

1. In the United States, there are fewer households comprised of mom, dad, and the kids than of single people living on their own. About 31 million Americans live alone. [Update: As of 2016, there were 35.4 million Americans living alone, and 1-person households comprised 28.1 percent of all households. In 1940, just 7.7 percent of all households included just one person.]

2. Have you heard the one about how single people need to "settle down"? Well, singles living solo are already settled. Follow them, and people in other household types, over a five-year period and you will find that the solo-dwellers are one of the most stable types.

3. Do you think that living solo is mostly for the very young adults and the very old (typically women who have outlived their husbands)? Wrong on both counts. The majority of people living on their own are between the ages of 35 and 65.

4. The percentage of single-person households in the U.S. is high. But the 28% figure is far outpaced by the 40 to 45% of single-person households in Sweden, Norway, Finland, and Denmark. In Stockholm, almost two-thirds of all households consist of just one person.

5. Living alone is not the same as feeling alone or isolated. In fact, "cities with high numbers of singletons enjoy a thriving public culture." If you live solo in a city and want to be with other people, often you can just walk out the door.

6. Although people who live alone often value solitude, the rise of solo living did not actually grow out of transcendental or monastic traditions. Instead, the culture and popularity of city living is the more significant factor.

7. Most old people who live alone do not do so because they have no grown children or anyone else who cares about them. It is their preference.

8. Solo dwellers are not just renters. Increasingly, they are buying homes of their own. "In the 1950s, real estate agents would have been surprised to see a single female client in their office; now it's surprising if they don't."

9. Holed up with your cat? Maybe. But people who live in couples or families are actually more likely to have a pet than people who live alone.

10. A few years ago, a bash-the-solo-dwellers story rippled through the media. The claim was that people living solo are taking up more resources per person than those who live in nuclear family homes. That can happen, but "Manhattan, the capital of American singleton society, is also the nation's greenest city." How can that be? Consider that "a family of four with two cars, long commutes, and a 2,500 square-foot house in the suburbs will leave a greater carbon footprint than four individual city dwellers who live in compact apartments and use public transportation (or, better, walk) to reach work."

11. Living alone is a norm and not an oddity, and that's something new in the world. "Today our species has about 200,000 years of experience with collective living, and only about fifty or sixty years with our experiment in going solo."

# 42

# Best Things About Living Alone

Living alone is one of my things, so "best things about living alone" lists can lure me in the way most other listicles cannot. I've read lots of them. But here's the thing: I think they are for lightweights. And I think they are written by people who, deep down inside, do not really get it about the profound fulfillment of the solo-dwelling life. It's different for those of us who really mean it about wanting to live alone.

Consider the supposedly best things about living single as offered up by the lightweights from places such as _Cosmo_ and _Buzzfeed_:

1. "You can use the bathroom without closing the door."

2. "You can stay up as long as you want. Without keeping it down for other people. Blast that episode of _Frasier_!"

3. "Nobody will steal your food."

4. "You can leave your clothes on the floor..."

5. "You can do all the embarrassing and gross things you want without fear of judgment."

6. "...you don't ever have to wear pants."

7. "You don't have to worry about a roommate hearing you have sex, or vice versa."

8. "You never have to wait for anyone to get out of the bathroom to pee or shower."

9. "You can use all the hot water in the shower."

10. "You don't have to share the TV..."

All these kinds of things are perfectly fine reasons for enjoying the experience of living alone. But if they are the *only* kinds of reasons you like having a place of your own, then maybe you are not that serious about it. The reasons have a kind of defensiveness to them, as if you are trying to convince yourself that you really do like living alone. The reasons are mostly about freedom *from* constraints (you don't have to wear clothes, you don't have to share) and when they are about freedom *to do* things (stay up as long as you want), what is enabled by that freedom is trivial (watch reruns of *Frasier*).

I like watching TV as much as the next person, but the freedom to do so is not among the most profound rewards of staying up as long as you want. Think about people who are really passionate about what they do. When they get engrossed in whatever it is that really grabs them – whether it is writing music or solving an intriguing problem or creating something or anything else – they love the freedom to just keep going. *It is a joy to stay engaged*, to go for hours without ever wondering about the time, to be free of concern about what some other person in the house thinks of you or wishes you were doing instead.

That's one of the real rewards of solo living for those who really mean it about wanting to live alone. Here are a few others:

- Other people are distracting and not just when they are talking to you or playing obnoxious music or watching annoying TV. The mere presence of other people can sap some of your emotional and intellectual resources. If someone else is around, a small part of you is paying attention to them. *When you live alone, you can think with your whole mind and feel with your whole heart.*

- People who really mean it about wanting to live alone *experience a sense of appreciation of a place of their own that is beyond the grasp of the causal solo dweller*. This is sometimes most apparent when they get their own place for the very first time. Even if the place is not all that great in objective ways (such as the size or the state of disrepair), people who crave living alone will savor and cherish it.

- For some people, living alone is not just a casual preference – it feels more like a need. What happens when you are deprived of a genuine need? You can't stop thinking about it. You daydream about it, makes plans for when you will get to have that need fulfilled again. When living alone is a need and you finally get to do it after being deprived, *you feel relief and a sense that your living situation is once again just what it should be.*

# Not Monitored, Not Judged:
# One of the True Joys of Living Alone?

I've never kept "normal" hours. I'm a night person, in the extreme. It is not unusual for me to be up until 3 a.m. My parents told me that even as an infant, I'd sleep all day and stay up all night.

I don't adhere to ordinary meal times, either. Sure, if I'm meeting someone for lunch or dinner, I'm happy to do so at a customary time. On my own, though, it's different.

I work at home most of the time and I like to wear sweats. If I'm reading for fun, I like to be sprawled out on the living room couch.

When I'm answering e-mails, cooking, puttering around, or doing other stuff that does not take up all my mental space, I often like to have the TV on in the background.

None of that is terribly embarrassing, I don't think, and anyway I just posted it on this blog that anyone with access to the internet can read. And yet, when I try to figure out what it is that I love so very much about living alone, I think it is, in part, the sense of not being monitored and not being judged.

To live single for your entire adult life in a society that is so matrimaniacal, it helps to be able to shrug off what other people think about how you are living your life. I have no problem with that. But on a day-to-day, moment-to-moment basis, I really appreciate the freedom from thinking about what other people are thinking about what I'm doing.

I know that other people have just the opposite preference. This past summer, I had lunch with a woman who was sharing a house with a man, just as roommates. She said that in the middle of the night, when she heard him coughing in the other room, she liked that reassurance that someone else was around. I like it that when I cough in the middle of the night, no one else hears me.

The freedom from feeling monitored or judged is not the only thing I love about living single, but I think it is a big one. I wonder how many others feel the same way.

# The Least Appreciated Perk of Living Alone

If you love your solitude and your own space, no one needs to persuade you of the joys of living alone. There is one particular perk of going solo, though, that seems to get less recognition than it deserves.

I realized this as I was reading a book that is more than 30 years old, Dolores Hayden's "*The Grand Domestic Revolution: A History of Feminist Designs for American Homes, Neighborhoods, and Cities*." One of the themes is that isolated homes and a gender-based division of labor leave women stuck with a lot of household drudgery. I hadn't known that there was a whole history of ideas and advocacy for ways of reducing chores. One of the chapters, for example, is titled "Homes without kitchens and towns without housework."

Enlisting men to do their share of the housework has been a goal of many women for a very long time. Even as traditional gender roles have lost much of their dominance, battles over household chores have not subsided. Popular writings and scholarly articles continue to address this source of conflict and stress.

If you live alone, though, you are blissfully free of such discord. Sure, you might wish that someone else would swoop in and clean your mess, or you might wish that you were more organized or that you had the money to hire a cleaning service. But you are not keeping tabs on what the other people living with you are doing and stewing when you think it is not enough. Nor are you feeling guilty when your own sense of acceptable orderliness falls below the standards of a spouse or roommate.

The freedom to be as neat or as messy as you like is not the most important perk of living solo, but it does deserve its due.

# 45

# How Living Alone Will Transform Men

Writings about single life – both popular and academic – focus overwhelmingly on women. Because marriage, traditionally, is supposed to be more important to women than to men, in theory more central to their identities and their happiness, single life should be especially problematic for women. Research begs to disagree about the happiness presumption, but no matter. Angst-filled writings about women living single continue to proliferate.

Alongside the tired old tales of those "poor" single women is a counter-narrative. It is one of strength, fulfillment, and independence. That story is often told of single women who live alone.

By living alone instead of with a husband and children, women are liberated from traditional roles and expectations. They are no longer the short-order cook, the cleaner-upper, and the laundress for a house full of family. They are freed of the emotional work of shoring up egos and soothing bruised feelings. They don't have to account to someone else for the money they spend. They also learn how to do the kinds of things that husbands traditionally did – or they find someone else to hire or to help.

What is less often noticed is what men get out of living alone. That has changed with Lynn Jamieson and Roona Simpson's academic book, _Living Alone: Globalization, Identity and Belonging_. They point out that as more and more men (and women) live alone in their early adult years, they are learning all sorts of skills that used to be the bailiwick of the other gender. In married life, for example, women were traditionally the "kinkeepers" and the social schedulers. They kept in touch with family, kept up with friends (if the friends had not been ditched), arranged social gatherings, and covered all the other socioemotional tasks of the couple.

In their interviews with people living alone and in their review of the relevant writings, the authors found that most young men living alone are doing just fine. They have networks of friends and relatives and keep in touch with the people who are important to them. They don't need a wife to have a social life or meaningful human connections.

That is important in and of itself. But it is also significant for what it suggests about the future. Right now, if you study people who live alone, as the authors and others have done, what you typically find is that most solo dwellers are doing fine. There is an exception, though – when there are people who conform to the stereotype of the sad, lonely, and isolated person living alone, those people are disproportionately older men, particularly those who are unemployed or in poor health. Maybe today's young men, when they get a lot older, will do a lot better if they live alone. They will already know how to have a good life while going solo.

# How People Will Try to Scare You About Being Alone – and Why You Should Blow Them Off

# 46

# I've Been Single All My Life.
# I Rarely Get Lonely.

Because I'm single and live alone, people who don't know me very well sometimes wonder whether I lead a lonely life. I can tell you exactly how long I can spend completely alone, with no face-to-face contact with any other humans, before I feel lonely: 15 days. I know because I tried it.

It wasn't meant to be an experiment in loneliness. I thought I was giving myself the gift of a writing retreat: I had read about writers who isolate themselves in a charming beach house in a deserted seaside town, and it was easy for me to create my own version. I was working on my latest book, and I already lived on my own in a little beach town. The isolation took care of itself; conveniently, the friends I see most often were all preoccupied at the time with traveling or caring for an ailing parent or some such.

The first week was pure bliss. During the second, I started to miss meaningful interactions with other people, but I was still mostly fine. But then I was done.

In my day-to-day life, I rarely feel lonely. Instead, I revel in solitude, savoring long hours of immersion in reading, writing, cooking, Netflix or whatever else calls out to me. I enjoy my friends, too. I don't socialize much with people I don't care about, so most of my time with others is engaging and warm, or neutral at worst. Afterward, though, I love returning to my empty, quiet home.

Because loneliness is the pain of missing out on the relationship experiences you wish you had, the remedy should be more quality time with other people. When my fanciful writer's retreat turned into a lonely abyss, it took the return of my friends to pull me out of it.

Yet for less acute experiences, I can recover nicely in other ways. A long walk on the beach or bluffs, or some verdant trail, might begin with sadness or stress, but it will almost always end with peacefulness and calm. Intellectual absorption works for me, too. When I first moved to Charlottesville and knew no one other than the people I had met briefly during my job interview, I spent most of my second evening writing a scholarly article, surrounded by rooms full of unpacked boxes.

I've been single all my life. According to prevailing cultural narratives, loneliness should not have to work so hard to catch me. As part of our research on perceptions of single people, my colleagues and I created biographical profiles and asked study participants for their impressions. The people in the profiles were described in identical ways, except that half the time, the profile was said to be of a single person, and the other half, a married one. Sometimes we described the person in the profiles as 25 years old and other times as 40. Participants routinely judged the single people as lonelier than the married people, and they thought the single people were especially lonely if they were 40 instead of 25.

Those impressions are most likely wrong. I've scoured academic journals for relevant studies, and I cannot find even one that shows that people who get married become less lonely than they were when they were single. But there *is* research showing that people who marry become less connected to friends and family than they were before. Although definitive long-term studies have not yet been conducted, the available evidence suggests that single people become more comfortable over time with their single lives, not less so.

Surely there are single people who are chronically lonely, just as there are married people who feel the same way. Yet the stereotypes that insist that *single* means *lonely* gloss over the diversity of experiences among the 107 million adults (in the United States alone) who are not married. Researchers have examined the psychological profiles of people who are afraid to be single, and people who like spending time alone. Both sets of studies show the same thing: People who are *not* afraid to be single and people who like spending time alone are less likely to experience loneliness. They are psychologically strong in other ways, too. For example, they are less likely to be neurotic and more likely to be open to new experiences.

My own interest is in people who are single at heart — those who live their best, most authentic and most meaningful lives by living single. My preliminary findings suggest that people who are single at heart don't worry about being lonely; instead, they embrace solitude. What's painful for all of these different types of people is not time alone but not having enough of it.

Reports about the dire consequences of loneliness seem to be proliferating, which is curious considering that, at least among high school and college students, loneliness has been declining for decades. I think the stories are expressing the kinds of fears that always bubble up in the midst of profound social changes. As the sociologist and author Eric Klinenberg has noted, the past half century marked "the first time in human history [when] great numbers of people ... have begun settling down as singletons."

I do think that loneliness should be taken seriously. For people whose loneliness is searing and relentless, concern is appropriate. But be cautious about swooping in to save those you only believe to be lonely because they are single or live alone. Those people may already feel liberated by the life they've chosen to live.

[Originally published in the *Washington Post*]

# Is a Solitary Life a Lonely Life?
# It Could Be Just the Opposite.

In a book called *Loneliness*, the authors describe their concern that Western societies are not taking seriously enough the inherent gregariousness of humans. They note that "the latest figures show that ever-greater numbers of people are accepting a life in which they are physically, and perhaps emotionally, isolated from one another." Among the evidence they cite in support of that fear is the growing number of people who live alone.

It seems intuitive that people who live alone would be lonelier than people who live with others. Most single people do not live alone, yet single people are believed to be lonelier than married people. I've found that in my own research, and other researchers in other countries have also found evidence for that stereotype.

A new study of loneliness, based on a large, nationally representative sample of German adults, allowed for tests of the link between loneliness, living alone, and living single. The research was based on data collected at one point in time (2013) from more than 16,000 Germans ranging in age from 18 to 103. The participants were from more than 10,000 households.

The authors found that when they compared people who lived alone to people who lived with others, in a way that allowed them to focus on that key aspect of their living arrangement without letting other factors muddy the picture, *the people who lived alone were less lonely*.

They also tried to make the case that single people are lonelier, and seemed to imply that if only they would get married, their loneliness would subside. But they ended up showing that they really don't understand some basic methodological issues, and they also don't appreciate, psychologically, how the experience of living single after you get divorced or become widowed could differ profoundly from the experience of living single all your life.

## Loneliness and Living Alone: The Link Is Not What You Think

When the authors simply compared the people who lived alone with those who lived with others, the people who lived alone did report more loneliness. But people who live alone differ from the people who live with others in all sorts of ways, so we don't know, without looking more closely, if living alone really is linked with greater loneliness.

Fortunately, the authors did look more closely. They found that one way that people living alone differed from others was in their income. So they controlled for income statistically. That means that they essentially compared people at the same level of income, to see how loneliness differed between those living alone and those living with others.

Here's what they found: When people living alone have the same income as people living with others, the people living alone are LESS lonely.

The authors concede that "living alone may even have beneficial effects on the quality of one's social relationships" and add, as researchers often do, that more research is needed. If they had not been so sure of the wonder of marriage, maybe they would have been familiar with the relevant research. Studies have already shown the ways in which single people are more connected to other people than married people are, and demonstrated that it is the people who marry, rather than those who stay single, who become more insular.

The research does *not* show that living alone is a cure for loneliness. Among the people who live alone are many (we don't know exactly how many) who *chose* to live that way. If people who prefer living with other people were urged to live alone, we don't know what would happen. Maybe they would make an effort to form and maintain the kinds of social ties that keep loneliness at bay. Or maybe they would just end up lonely.

## What the Authors Don't Understand about the Link Between Loneliness and Single Life

The authors used their big dataset to compare three groups: (1) people who are single and not living with a partner; (2) people who have a romantic partner but are not living together; and (3) people who are living with a romantic partner (and are often married).

They think they know what they are going to find, because in their view, previous research has shown that "Being married is robustly associated with lower levels of loneliness." They then report that in their own research, "average loneliness levels were highest among singles and lowest among those living with their partners."

You could be forgiven for thinking that the authors are trying to tell us something more: that if only those poor single people would get married, their loneliness would dissipate. The authors never quite say that married people are less lonely *because* they are married, but that seems to be the implication.

The problem is, neither their data, nor the data from the previous research they cite, could ever establish that getting married caused people to be less lonely. In fact, the design of the studies and the comparisons they use are a set-up, biased to make married people look less lonely than they really are. The studies compare only those people who are currently married (or living with a romantic partner) to those who are single. They set aside all the people who got married, felt desperately lonely in their marriage, and then got divorced. No, wait – the authors of this paper did not set them aside. If the people who got divorced are still single, the authors included them in the single group, along with the lifelong single people.

And what about all the people who are widowed, and who may indeed feel deeply lonely without their spouse? They are tossed in with the lifelong single people, too.

So, here's what their data really did show: If you include in the group of single people all the people who are widowed (and may well be quite lonely) as well as all the people who chose to marry but then divorced (and may also be feeling lonely on their own after having been married), then yes, the people who are left in the married group are less lonely than all the people who got tossed into the single group. But does that mean that if all the single people got married, they would become less lonely? No, the research does not show that at all.

In fact, even using the cheater technique that gives married people a great big unfair advantage, the results were a lot less definitive than the authors expected. When they looked separately at the three age groups, they found that romantic relationship status just didn't matter among the adults who were younger than 30. People who were living with a romantic partner (and often married), people who had a partner but were not living with that partner, and people who were single (they had no romantic partner) all experienced about the same levels of loneliness.

Among those older than 65, the singles were a bit lonelier, but the differences were small. Only among the middle-aged group (30-65) were the people living with romantic partners noticeably less lonely than the single people.

The authors want you to think that they were less lonely *because* they were married (or cohabiting). They don't want you to even consider the possibility that the married group looks less lonely because so many of the people who were lonely in their marriages got divorced (and then the authors put them in with the lifelong single people). They don't want you to think too much about the fact that the single group also includes people who are widowed, and are probably lonely because they miss their spouse. They just want you to think: single = lonely; married = not lonely.

I want you to think smarter than that.

So, when the authors said, in the abstract (summary) of their article, that the "late-life increase in loneliness could be explained by...higher proportion of singles in this age group," they want you to think that single = lonely. They want you to think, oh those poor old people, they are lonely because they are single. But maybe they are lonely because so many of them are widowed. Maybe they spent so many years of their lives married that they don't know how to lead a full, rich, socially connected life as a single person. And maybe lifelong single people do know how to do that.

No need to qualify that last statement with a "maybe." As I already mentioned, we already know, from lots of research, that lifelong single people have more friends than married people, and do more to maintain their ties with friends, siblings, parents, and neighbors. It is when people get married that they turn inward and pay less attention to the people in their lives other than their spouse.

### Clinging to Ideological Beliefs, Not Scientific Facts

The authors seem to believe in the ideology of marriage which maintains that just about everyone wants to marry and that people who get married become better off physically, psychologically, and interpersonally than they were when they were single. My guess is that they have never even thought to question those ideological assumptions.

I say that because of the way they talk about single people and partnered people. For example:

- When discussing loneliness in older people, they say that "the absence of a significant attachment figure (spouse, partner)" is important. Do you see what's wrong with that? To the authors, only a spouse or romantic partner counts as a significant attachment figure. No matter how close you may be to a lifelong friend, a sibling, or anyone else; and no matter if your relationship with another person meets all the criteria for an attachment relationship – the authors still don't think your attachment figure is significant if that person is not a spouse or romantic partner.

- The authors say that "the formation of an intimate relationship and partnership in young adults is a developmental accomplishment." It is, if that's what you want. And the authors seem to believe that everyone wants that. But they are wrong. There are young adults (and adults of every age) who are uninterested in that goal. In the authors' opinion, marriage is an accomplishment, and they are passing off that ideological belief as a statement of fact in a scientific publication.

- When the authors find, to their surprise, that romantic relationship status has nothing to do with loneliness among adults younger than 30, they try to explain it this way: "...younger people can compensate for the absence of a romantic partner through a larger social network in both private and professional life." The key word is "compensate." It reveals the authors' assumption that romantic relationships matter more than any other relationships, to all people, and therefore if adults do not have such a relationship, they need to "compensate" for that somehow.

The compensation mindset is especially remarkable in light of the authors' own findings. Relationship status did not matter as much as they thought it would (and probably wanted it to). Results were not consistent across the three age groups, and they did not mean what the authors said they did. But another factor did matter, in predictable ways, and in consistent ways across the three age groups: having friends. What's more, there was no undermining the importance of friendship, no matter how the authors analyzed the data. People with more friends were less lonely. The results were that simple. But nowhere do we hear anything about how people need to "compensate" for not having friends.

# Are Americans Becoming More and More Isolated?
# Debunking a Claim that Went Viral

First, let's talk about you. Then we'll get to everyone else. What are your answers to these two questions:

1. Looking back over the last six months – who are the people with whom you discussed matters important to you?

2. How many friends outside of your household do you have that you see or speak to at least once a week?

## The Latest Media Panic about Lonely, Isolated Americans

In 2006, a media panic broke out over a report about the answers to question #1. Maybe you remember some of the headlines – they were everywhere. For example:

"Americans' circle of friends is shrinking, new study shows" (from *Science Daily*)

"The lonely American just got a little bit lonelier" (from the *New York Times*)

"Study: 25% of Americans have no one to confide in" (from *USA Today*)

The study that ignited the panic had just been published in a prestigious sociology journal. Authors <u>McPherson, Smith-Lovin, and Brashears</u> reported the results of a nationally representative survey of approximately 1,500 Americans. The data were collected in 2004, and compared to the answers to a similar survey from 1985.

The findings appeared to show that Americans had become dramatically more isolated over the course of the two decades. In 1985, 10% answered "no one" to the first question. By 2004, nearly 25% (24.9%, to be exact, according to the first report) said that there was no one with whom they had discussed important matters in the past six months.

The average number of people that Americans named in response to that question dropped, too. In 1985, it was about 3 people; by 2004, it was just 2. That's a decrease of about one-third – by sociological standards, a huge change over a relatively short historical period.

To many, the case was made. Americans were growing increasingly isolated. Pundits scurried to their keyboards to offer their favorite explanations and forebodings. More than a few scholars also accepted that conclusion. But was it really true?

## Other Perspectives and More Data

In the abstract of their original journal article, McPherson and his colleagues noted that "the data may overestimate the number of social isolates." The group in charge of the survey (NORC) looked more closely at the data and found some errors that rendered the results slightly less striking but the significant trends remained.

Some of the most eminent scholars of the study of social networks, including Claude Fischer and Barry Wellman, were skeptical. Just last year, the same journal (American Sociological Review) published a critical analysis by Fischer, as well as a response from the McPherson team. Some of the disagreements were about the proper statistical models to use and whether it is plausible that Americans' social connections could have changed so much in so short a time. Fischer believes there may have been a technical error (for example, in the devices used to record participants' answers). It is not clear whether we will ever know for sure what to think of the 2004 data that launched countless "lonely American" essays.

To me, it seems most productive to look at other data, both within the same surveys, and perhaps more compellingly, from entirely different surveys. Fischer reported that within the same surveys, answers to other questions did not seem to paint a picture of increasingly isolated Americans. For example, when asked how often they spend a social evening with neighbors, relatives, or friends beyond the neighborhood, the answers changed hardly at all from 1985 to 2004. The same was true for answers to the question, "How many close friends would you say you have?" The number did not shrink over time. The McPherson team responded that the questions were measuring different kinds of social ties, so in their opinion, there was no contradiction.

Now let's return to the second question I posed at the beginning of this article: "How many friends outside of your household do you have that you see or speak to at least once a week?" Hua Wang and Barry Wellman analyzed the answers to that question (and others), as posed in two other national surveys – one from 2002 and another from 2007.

Wang and Wellman found that in both 2002 and 2007, only 5% of American adults said that they had no friends they saw or spoke to at least once a week. (Remember that McPherson reported that nearly 25% of Americans were isolated in 2004.) The friendship study authors also computed the median number of friends, and found that it was either 5 or 6. In their words:

> "The average number of friends contacted face-to-face and by phone was substantial early in the decade, and it continued to be substantial. The number of friendships did not decline. Rather, it increased on average between 2002 and 2007 and increased the most for heavy Internet users."

Other studies (described in Fischer's 2009 article and the Wang and Wellman paper) also suggest that Americans are not nearly as isolated as McPherson claimed. The latter team might again say that the questions are not the same – the number of people with whom you discuss important matters is not the same as the number of friends you see or talk to at least once a week. That may be so. Still, the weight of the evidence does not seem to support sweeping statements about how already-lonely Americans have become alarmingly more isolated.

## If You've Studied Social History, This May All Sound Familiar

Media panics about social isolation are nothing new. To quote Wang and Wellman again:

> "Putnam (2000) looked back nostalgically from the 1990s to the 1960s and argued that Americans were 'bowling alone' because television watching was keeping people from community involvement. Likewise, in the 1960s, Stein (1960) and Nisbet looked back to the 1930s and mourned the decline of social connectivity. Yet in the 1930s, Wirth (1938) looked to preurban America and worried about the loss of social connectivity in transitory urban life."

Undoubtedly, many Americans are lonely, and their distress should not be dismissed or trivialized. But nor should the number of lonely people be overstated.

I just want to mention two other points that are not always acknowledged. Consider, once again, question #1: In the past 6 months, "who are the people with whom you discussed matters important to you?" The question was NOT, "are there people with whom you COULD have discussed important matters if you had wanted to do so?"

In contemporary American society, many people value openness and communication and having close friends. I'm often one of them. We should not forget, though, that other people are not as fond of emotional sharing. Just because a certain manner of relating, or a certain kind of social connectedness, is generally a good thing does not mean that it is the ideal way of being for every single person.

My second point is perhaps less plausible, and I'm not sure I believe it myself, but I'll put it out there anyway. If there is a real trend showing that people are less likely to discuss important matters with others than they were in the past, maybe that means that their lives have improved. The kinds of important matters were the highly educated. Education is often linked to better financial status. Economic disparities have increased over time in the United States. Maybe the better-off Americans just didn't have as many important matters to discuss with others.

# Isolated People Who Are Not Lonely and Connected People Who Are: A 20-Year Study

One of the biggest misconceptions about loneliness is that people who are "isolated" according to some objective measure (for example, they live alone) must also be lonely. The converse produces its own common misunderstanding – that if you are connected to others in some objective way (for example, you are married and live with your spouse), then you are probably not lonely.

Statistically, we can show that isolation and loneliness are not perfectly correlated. A pair of researchers from Wales went far beyond that. In 1979, they recruited 500 people from rural Wales who were at least 65 years old and followed them for the next 20 years. They interviewed them in their homes every four years, asking standard questions about isolation and loneliness, as well as other open-ended questions about their lives.

By 1999, there were only 47 people who were still alive and not living in an institution, so that small sample size needs to be kept in mind.

To be considered socially **isolated**, more than one of the following had to apply:

- Lives alone

- Never goes out of the house

- Has no close relatives

- Never visits anyone

- Has no contact with neighbors

- Is alone for more than 9 hours a day

- Has no telephone

- Nearest neighbor is more than 50 yards away (out of earshot)

To determine **loneliness**, the researchers used these criteria:

- Feels lonely much of the time

- Wishes for more friends

- Does not see enough of friends and relatives

- Has no confidant

- Has no real friends living nearby

- Does not meet enough people

- Has no one of whom to ask favors

- Spent the previous Christmas alone *and* lonely

Let's consider the people who were classified objectively as isolated, but who were not lonely. What were they like?

## Isolated but Not Lonely

- They are people who enjoy their own company. They tend to be quiet or reserved.

- Either they have satisfying relationships with friends or neighbors, or they have always stayed to themselves

- In this sample, they were all people who did not have children

- They have self-sufficient personalities

- They spent the previous Christmas alone by choice

Some people were isolated or lonely early in the study but overcame their loneliness later on. Typically, these were people who had made lifestyle changes. For example, one person, at the outset of the study, had been recently widowed. Twelve years later, though, she had made several good friends and also had good relationships with neighbors; she was no longer lonely. Another example involved a widowed farmer who was initially very isolated and lonely. After suffering a heart attack, he cut down on the number of livestock he maintained, and spent more time chatting with neighbors and hanging out at the pub. He wasn't lonely any more, either.

Now let's look at the people who did not qualify as isolated but did score as lonely.

**Not Isolated but Lonely**

- They are caring for a dependent spouse and have little help

- They are living with an adult child who is working full time

- They have experienced the death of their spouse or friends

- They moved during the study

- Their health is deteriorating

- No one visits them

- They don't ask for help

I expected this category to include people who were living with another person and not getting along very well with that person. However, there was no mention of that.

After presenting their findings, the authors shared their thoughts about possible policy changes or interventions. The last few sentences of the article were these:

> "...it would be wrong to assume that solitude should always be a target for intervention and change. Solitude may be associated with a greater risk of undiscovered emergencies, but it is probably the risk that should be reduced and not the solitude itself, which may be cherished."

**Reference**: Wenger, G. C., & Burholt, V. (2004). Changes in levels of social isolation and loneliness among older people in a rural area: A twenty-year longitudinal study. *Canadian Journal on Aging*, 23, 115-127.

# 50

## But What If You *Are* Lonely?

Loneliness has a prominent place in the news these days. As the number of people who live alone continues to grow, as does the number of seniors, concern swells. Studies suggesting all sorts of dire correlates of loneliness increase the worry to a state of near panic.

Neither living alone nor growing old means that you will end up lonely. Loneliness is different from living alone or spending time alone. Many people, including most who are single at heart, savor their solitude. Loneliness is not about savoring, it is about pain. It is the distress we feel when our social relationships are not what we want them to be. People can feel deeply lonely when they are in a marriage and when they are in a crowd.

Because loneliness is so painful, it needs to be taken seriously. Yet as psychologists, it is worth stepping back and asking whether any good can come from experiencing loneliness. Recently, several writers have dared to suggest that the answer is yes.

Jessica Crispin is one of them. In a beautifully-written opinion piece in the *New York Times*, "St. Teresa and the Single Ladies," Crispin suggests:

*"But loneliness and vulnerability can be tools, if you can stand the pressure of them. Loneliness awakens not only your attention, as you scan rooms in the hopes of finding someone to alleviate it, but it also drives your empathy."*

The brilliant author and social critic, Vivian Gornick, also described the power and the potential in loneliness in her essay in the *Nation*, "The Dread of Loneliness":

*"...loneliness, once demystified, is not only not fatal, it can be a source of revelation. If you determined on not drowning in it – that is, if you swam steadily against the current – you discovered a power of survival you'd never have thought part of your psychic apparatus."*

I'm a true believer in research-based conclusions, so I see personal essays such as Crispin's and Gornick's as sources of intriguing hypotheses rather than evidence for the positive possibilities in loneliness. They are wake-up calls to researchers to broaden their perspectives on the meanings of loneliness and other painful psychological experiences.

There are some telling precedents, such as what we learned from mountains of research on depression. Like loneliness, depression is a painful experience. Psychological research suggests that it is linked to other unfortunate outcomes. Yet, studies also showed that depressed people sometimes have special insights and sensitivities. For example, they can be more realistic in their appraisals of other people, when those who are not depressed are too quick to be taken in by what other people want them to believe.

I discovered that myself in research I did with people who were mildly depressed and those who were not depressed at all. My colleague Julie Lane and I played video and audio recordings of people in several studies who were being less than honest. In one of the studies, participants talked to an art student about her paintings, including a few that they really disliked. In another, college students tried to ingratiate themselves with other students. It was the mildly depressed people, rather than the people who were not depressed, who were particularly attuned to the false reassurances and the phoniness.

That doesn't mean I'd want to spend time feeling lonely or depressed. I wouldn't. But painful experiences of all sorts are not all bad. And that's a valuable thing to know.

**51**

# Spending Holidays Alone: The Saddest Thing Imaginable or Totally Badass?

Just before Thanksgiving, NPR posted a question on its website asking people to weigh in about spending holidays alone. Are they doing so themselves and why?

NPR got a flood of answers. From my perch as a practitioner and scholar of single life, what I found most intriguing was the range of responses. My guess is that if NPR had posed this question three or four decades ago, the reactions would have been overwhelmingly negative – people appalled at the idea of spending a holiday alone, or pitying those who do. People who were planning to be alone perhaps would have been reluctant to say so.

The online question did elicit some darkness ("This is the saddest thing NPR has ever posted"), some accusations ("You must hate people if you are choosing to be alone on Thanksgiving"), and some defensiveness. But another category of responses was entirely different. People talked about how much they enjoyed being alone.

Law student Laura Thornton, for example, told NPR that her plan was to:

*"just chill out with my dog and drink whiskey in my apartment, like I did last Thanksgiving. Sometimes I find it hard to take time out for myself, so it's actually kind of nice to have this time imposed on me. Plus, hopefully I'll get a lot of work done."*

True confessions: I was quoted in the story. Because I wrote out my thoughts about what I wanted to convey to the author of the story (Linton Weeks), I'd like to share the full text:

*At a time when too many people are feeling hyper-connected, overstimulated, too busy, and too hassled, what could be more dreamy than spending an entire day, completely on your own, doing whatever you want, whenever you want?*

*I suspect that if there were some real-life truth serum and it could be administered to people around the holidays, some not-too-small proportion of them would say that time to themselves is what they want most.*

*Not everyone would want this, of course. But I think the biggest impediment to people owning up to this particular fantasy is that it is not what we are supposed to want. Thanksgiving is one of those holidays that are highly scripted. You are supposed to spend it with other people – especially with family. All jokes and sitcoms aside, you are supposed to want to spend it that way. If you don't, the conventional wisdom goes, then you are some sort of loser.*

*Well, myth-busting is my thing, so let me shake down this one. If you really do want to spend Thanksgiving with family or friends, and you have the opportunity to do so, then go for it. But if you have that longing for solitude – if that's what really makes your heart sing – then go for that. Then own your decision; don't apologize for it. One person doing what they most want to do can be an inspiration to others who would like to do the same, but need a little nudge.*

*I'm an eclectic when it comes to Thanksgiving. I've tried out so many permutations – the traditional extended family version, the friends-only variation, and the time-alone variety; I've hosted anywhere from one to more than a dozen at my home, I've gone to others' homes, and I've traveled to a place I've never been before; I've trudged through snow one year and enjoyed dinner on the beach the next.*

*This year, I'm celebrating Thanksgiving on my own. I'll sleep late, and if it is a typical sunny day here in southern California, I'll walk the beach or one of the breath-taking trails. My computer, my email, and all other electronic devices will be off all day. I love to cook, so maybe I'll make a few things I love. I'll probably read a novel all the way through without having to set it aside again and again because I think I need to get some work done. Or I could have a Netflix night – or maybe both.*

*And here's the thing about celebrating a holiday your own way: If I wake up and decide that I feel like doing something else entirely, well then I'll just do that instead.*

# 52

## Aging on Your Own:
## 5 Things They Never Tell You When They Try to Scare You

Oh, to be old and on your own. That used to be one of the media's favorite scare stories. To some extent, it still is. The reality, though, is a whole lot different. Over the past half-century or so, what it means to be aging on your own has been changing dramatically – in many ways, for the better.

The Council on Contemporary Families (CCF) released a report called "Aging alone in America." It was written by Eric Klinenberg (author of *Going Solo*), Stacy Torres, and Elena Portacolone.

Here are some of questions and conclusions from the CCF report.

### #1. Why are more older Americans on their own? It is not just about women outliving their husbands.

If the educated layperson knows one thing about the demographics of aging, it is that women live longer than men and so in later life, the women who have outlived their husbands are often living on their own. That's true. And, of course, some Americans are on their own in later life because they never did marry.

There's another factor, too, and this one was news to me. I have been hearing for a long time that the divorce rate has leveled off – it is no longer increasing. What I didn't know was how different the numbers are by age. From the CCF report:

"While divorce rates have fallen for younger Americans over the past 30 years, *the divorce rate for people over 65 has doubled since 1990*."

## #2. But why are they *living* alone?

Just because you are widowed or divorced or have always been single does not mean that you are living on your own – in your own place, shared by no one else. Increasingly, though, more and more older Americans are living just that way.

Consider, for example, this striking reversal, as described in the CCF report:

"One hundred years ago, 70 percent of American widows and widowers moved in with their families. Today nearly the same proportion of widows and widowers live alone."

Why the change? Because it is what older people want. Staying in their own places – now called "aging in place" – is their first choice of how to live. That is so even when their grown kids want to take them in, a willingness that has actually increased in the most recent generation.

## #3. Money is the enabler and the disabler.

There is another crucial reason why more seniors are living on their own – they can afford to. The poverty rate among the elderly had fallen dramatically over time. Thank-you, Social Security. Thank-you, Medicare.

Of course, when it comes to economic resources, not all seniors are equal. Here are some groups especially likely to struggle financially in later life:

A. Financially, aging *renters* have a harder time than aging homeowners. But even those who have fully paid for the homes that they own still have to pay property taxes and cover any maintenance and repair expenses that come up.

B. Older *women* are more likely to be living in poverty than older men, 10.7 percent compared to 6.6 percent.

C. *Black* and *Hispanic* women who live alone are particularly likely to be poor, 38 percent and 41 percent, respectively.

**#4.** <u>Nora Ephron may have felt badly about her neck</u>, **but other body parts are not what we expect**.

If you live alone and you have serious health problems, that will be difficult. No sugar coating. But the odds of that happening are actually dropping. Again, from the CCF report:

"Disability rate have been falling. And a 2009 Pew Research Center survey found that the percentage of young and middle-aged adult who expected to experience problems associated with old age such as memory loss, serious illness, or lack of sexual activity was much higher than the percentage of older adults who reported actually dealing with these issues."

**#5. In *Singled Out*, I made fun of the myth that "you will grow old alone and you will die in a room by yourself where no one will find you for weeks." The CCF report agrees that many of these scare stories are myths**.

I have often discussed the studies showing that <u>people who are single are more often in touch with other people such as friends and neighbors</u>, compared to those who are married. The CCF report underscores that the same is true if you look just at the older people who are living alone.

Women, especially, seem to do well on their own in later life:

"A 2007 study funded by the Economic and Social Research Council found that women over sixty who lived alone expressed more happiness with their lives than married women of the same age."

# 53

# Will You Grow Old Alone If You Are Single? The Not-Very-Scary Results from 6 Nations

You know the <u>scare story</u> – if you are single, you will grow old alone. I'll take that scare story and raise it – if you are single and have no children, you will surely grow old alone. Not!

Scholars have been remiss in mostly neglecting the study of adults who have no children, and especially, within that category, adults who have always been single. Within the past few years, though, a wonderful collection of datasets from as many as 9 different countries has begun to be mined. The participating scholars have looked into all sorts of questions about adults with no children. Here, I'd like to tell you what they've learned about the social support networks of older people who have always been single and have no children.

**Complete information on social networks could be culled from six of the countries:**

- Australia

- Finland

- The Netherlands

- Spain

- The UK

- The US

All the participants were at least 65 years old. The key question that motivated the authors was whether these older people, who had been single all their lives and had no children, would have the kinds of restrictive social support networks that would leave them vulnerable in their later lives. All For each country, the authors compared 12 groups: men without children, women without children, mothers and fathers – and within those groups, people who had always been single or were currently married or were previously married.

**Five different kinds of social support networks were identified. The first two are the most limited:**

1. *Local self-contained*: people with this type of network are mostly home-centered in their lives, reaching out to neighbors when necessary.

2. *Private restricted*: this very limited support network is typical of married couples who mostly look only to each other for support, only rarely connecting with locals for help.

**Less restricted than the first two are:**

3. *Local family dependent*: people with these networks have relatives nearby and they rely on them when they need help or support.

**In the last two types of social support networks, friends have important roles and other people do, too.**

4. *Locally integrated*: people with these networks have kin nearby who are part of their social networks, but friends and neighbors are also important to them.

5. *Wider community focused*: People with these networks have no relatives nearby, though if they do have kin, they stay in touch with them. Their social support networks include friends and members of local voluntary groups.

As you might imagine, with 6 different countries and 12 kinds of marital/parental groups and 5 types of social networks, the results can be complex. Still, amidst all the details, some telling patterns did emerge. Two of them characterize all the countries except Australia (which I'll discuss later).

First, adults with no children tended to have the most restricted networks – either local self-contained or private restricted.

Second, there was a big exception to the first conclusion. Women who had always been single and who had no children often had the kinds of support networks in which friends were important – either locally integrated networks (in which local kin and neighbors, as well as friends, were part of the everyday support system) or wider community focused networks (among those who had no relatives nearby).

In Australia, both the men and the women who had always been single were likely to have local self-contained networks. Among the other marital/parental groups, the wider community focused network was much more commonplace than it was in the other countries. The authors speculate that the huge size of the country, together with the low population density, may contribute to different results for Australians, but they don't really know for sure.

So are they vulnerable – those adults in later life who have always been single and have no children? The men in that category are more likely to have restricted networks than men in most other categories. Even for them, though, the vast majority of them (except in Australia) have support networks that are not restricted. Specifically, the **percentages** of always-single men with no children who have local self-contained networks are specified in the first number in the list below. (I'll explain the second later.)

**Percent** (%)

**59** for Australia (vs. **9**)

**31** for Finland (vs. **61**)

**28** for the Netherlands (vs. **36**)

**0** for Spain (vs. **18**)

**17** for the UK (vs. **43**)

**16** for the US. (vs. **30**)

The second number for each nation is the percentage of married men with no children who have private restricted networks. These men mostly rely on their spouse and no one else. That's a kind of vulnerability, too.

For the always-single women with no children, the answer to the question of whether they are growing old alone is a resounding no. They are especially likely to have locally integrated or wider community focused social support networks.

**Reference**: Wenger, G. C., Dykstra, P. A., Melkas, T., & Knipscheer, K. C. P. M. (2007). Social embeddedness and late-life parenthood: Community activity, close ties, and support networks. *Journal of Family Issues, 11*, 1419-1456.

# 54

## Is a Solitary Life a Shorter Life?
## Here's What's Wrong with That Claim

In just 11 pages, Julianne Holt-Lunstad and her colleagues reported a meta-analysis (statistical summary) of a vast amount of data on the question of whether loneliness or social isolation or living alone is a risk factor for living a shorter life. The review incorporated data from 70 studies and more than 3.4 million people who were followed for an average of 7 years.

An article about it in the *New York Times* began like this:

> "Do you like being alone? New research from Brigham Young University shows just how bad loneliness and social isolation, even for people who prefer their own company, can be for health."

Actually, it does not show that at all. The researchers *never compared people who did and did not like living alone* to see whether that factor mattered.

Here's what they actually did do. They looked for studies measuring loneliness, social isolation, and living alone and mortality. People who reported various degrees of loneliness and social isolation, and people who did and did not live alone were identified, and then researchers kept track of who was still living an average of 7 years later.

Loneliness, social isolation, and living alone are three different things, so it is good that the authors studied all three. Loneliness is subjective. It is typically measured with loneliness scales that include items such as "I feel completely alone", "I am unhappy doing so many things alone", and "I feel as if nobody really understands me." Loneliness is not the same as the amount of social contact you have with other people. It is about whether you get the amount and quality of interpersonal bonding that you desire. For example, married people and people who spend lots of time with other people can feel lonely, and single people and those who spend very little time with others can be mostly free of feelings of loneliness. (For the actual link between marital status and loneliness, check out, "Escape from loneliness: Is marriage the answer?)

The authors define "social isolation" as "pervasive lack of social contact or communication, participation in social activities, or having a confidant." It is measured objectively – for example, by asking lots of people about their contact and communications with others and classifying the people with the least as socially isolated. The definition of living alone is objective, too.

Results showed that the people who lived longer were those who were less socially isolated and less lonely and those who did not live alone. The finding that people who lived alone did not live as long as people who lived with others is probably what led the *New York Times* to wrongly proclaim that even if you like being alone, it is bad for your health. Averaging across the millions of participants, those who lived alone did not live as long as those who lived with others. But within the millions of people are some very important differences, and the implications of most of those differences were never assessed.

Here's a personal example. My mother lived with her parents until she married and lived with my father for the next 42 years until he died suddenly. Then, at age 65, she lived alone for the first time in her life. I was living alone at that time, too. Once I got past the college/grad school roommate phase, I chose to live alone for my entire adult life. I hope I always will get to live alone. I love going solo. If my mother and I were included in that review article right after my father died, we both would have been classified as living alone. Yet the psychology of living alone for her and for me could hardly be more different.

To try to make it even clearer why it matters that the researchers never compared those who like living alone to those who do not, I'll offer some hypothetical results. Suppose that across all the people living alone, 22 percent died during the 7 years they were studied, whereas only 20 percent of those not living alone died. Looks bad for those going solo. But now suppose we do what the researchers did not do – compare the half of the solo dwellers who most liked living alone to the half who least liked it. Hypothetically, 25 percent of the dislikers could have dropped dead over the 7-year period, compared to just 19 percent of those who live alone and love it. That would mean that the lovers of solo life actually *lived longer* than those who lived with other people, even though people who live alone in general (averaging across the likers and the dislikers) live less long than those who live with others. (The more appropriate analyses would separate the likers from the dislikers among both those who live alone and those who live with others. Surely there are people living with others who wish they were living alone.)

The problem with declaring that living alone is bad for your health, on the basis of the available research, is similar in some ways to the problem of declaring that being single (as compared to being married) is bad for your health. We cannot randomly assign people to be single or to be married – they get to choose. The people who choose to marry are different people than those who choose to stay single. What makes for a good or long life for someone who chooses to marry (or live with others) may be different from what makes for a good or long life for someone who chooses to stay single (or live alone).

The key question is this: If you took people who choose to live alone and who love living that way, and forced them to live with other people, would that prolong their lives? Or as the joke about marriage goes – do married people live longer, or does it just seem longer?

**Reference**: Holt-Lunstad, J., Smith, T. B., Baker, M., Harris, T., & Stephenson, D. (2015). Loneliness and social isolation as risk factors for mortality: A meta-analytic review. *Perspectives on Psychological Science, 10,* 227-237.

# 55

# The Ultimate Threat to Single People – You'll Die Alone

I'm not a regular viewer of the TV show, *Private Practice*, but I watched it last night. One of the storylines was about a man who was in the final stages of pancreatic cancer, in pain, and wanting to die. Two of the regular doctors on the show, Sam and Pete – described in the episode preview as old friends and colleagues of the dying man – clash over the ethics of facilitating the man's death.

On another matter, though, the two share an understanding that is so deep that it never occurs to either to question it: that the man, because he has no spouse, is "dying alone." They consider this tragic, and horribly unsettling, because they, too, are single. They are stricken with the fear that their own death could be akin to that of their long-time friend and colleague.

As the man lays dying, at home in his own bed, the two friends are sitting there near him. By the time his last breath is about to be drawn, Pete has climbed into bed with him, cradling him in his arms. That's where he dies.

This is *Private Practice*'s definition of "dying alone." It is many other people's as well. The usual perversion of the "alone" word is in play: If you have two old friends with you, one actually in bed with you and holding you in his arms, you have died alone. By this taken-for-granted definition, friends are not people. Unless there is a spouse present, you have died alone.

There is something stunningly clueless about the belief that if you marry, you will not die alone. First, a point that should be obvious: Unless both partners die instantaneously, someone is left "alone" (according to the dopey definition of "alone").

My parents were married for 42 years, and had four kids. My father died first. He was hospitalized because of some pain that had not yet been properly diagnosed. The cause turned out to be an abdominal aneurysm. It left him lying dead on the bathroom floor of his hospital room late at night, after my mother had gone home for the evening. All of us grown kids were by then living in other parts of the country. He really did die alone.

My mother, in the popular parlance, was then "alone." During the last five days of her life, as she was dying from cancer, all four of us kids were there with her, often sleeping in chairs or on the floor in the same room, leaving only occasionally to grab a quick shower or a bag of bagels to pass around. Her brother and a lifetime of relatives and friends wanted to be there, too, and they had visited many times before; during the last days, though, my sibs and I did not want to share.

It is true that some single people really do die alone, in the true sense of the word and not the sense that discounts everyone who is not a spouse. But as the example of my own father shows, so, too, do some people who are in the fifth decade of their only marriage, and have four grown children.

As Kay Trim Berger has noted, marital status may not be as powerful a predictor of whether you will die alone as whether you have maintained a circle of friends. In fact, the intensive coupling that some married partners practice (whereby all of the once-important people in their lives are moved to the back burner as the marital relationship becomes all-consuming) may be what leaves people particularly vulnerable to loneliness and dying alone when the marriage ends.

I have another challenge to the "Horrors: You'll Die Alone!" threat: Some people actually prefer to be alone, even in death. For a beautifully written example, read the afterword in the book *Party of One*, by Anneli Rufus.

Suppose, though, that you are not one of those people. Suppose you really do want people around you when you die. I'll even up the ante: Suppose you want a *spouse* there with you when you die. Still, I have to wonder: Should you let that wish for your final hours determine the fate of the rest of your life? Should you find someone to marry, even if you are not sure you really want to marry? Even if you do want to marry but have never found a person you truly want to spend your life with, should you marry someone who is a "good enough" partner just to have a spouse there with you at the end?

Answer any of these questions any way you like. Just don't accept the "die alone" threat unthinkingly. Let your life decisions be governed by your own beliefs and values and feelings, your sense of who you really are and who you want to be, and not by the mindless myths designed to scare or shame you out of your single state.

# 56

# Who Gets Spooked by Stories of Single People Dying Alone? It's Not Who You Think

There is a certain story told about single people that seems to have an odd sort of power. It is the story about a single person dying all alone, their body undiscovered for a very long time. Often, the person dies watching TV and when someone finally finds them – maybe because of the foul odor emanating from their apartment – the TV is still on. An addition indignity is sometimes added – insects are crawling all over the dead body, maybe even consuming it.

Many of these depictions are fictional. As sociologists Neta Yodovich and Kinneret Lahad point out in their scholarly analysis, they have shown up in TV shows such as *Bones, Sex and the City*, and *Six Feet Under*. Sometimes they make an appearance in humorous asides, as in the infamous quip from *Bridget Jones Diary* warning that single people could end up "dying alone and found three weeks later half-eaten by an Alsatian."

Once in a great while, some version of the scare story really does happen in real life – though usually not the part about getting eaten by critters. An example was a man who died in New York, whose story was described at great length by the *New York Times* in 2015. The article was immensely popular, staying atop the list of most-read stories for days.

I struggled with the appeal of that story at the time, and I'm still wondering about the psychological dynamics that draw people into these narratives. Why do single people read these stories? What about married people or people such as aging unmarried parents living with their grown children?

There are some easy answers that may or may not capture a bit of the truth. For example, maybe there are single people who have internalized the cultural scare stories and truly are frightened that they will die alone and their body will go undiscovered for months. And maybe the married people, and the unmarried people safely ensconced in comfortable homes with their children right there beside them, feel smugly superior when they hear those kinds of stories. Maybe they feel confident that such a dire fate will never befall them.

I've been thinking about this again after reading that intriguing sociological paper. The authors paid special attention to an episode from *Six Feet Under*, "The Invisible Woman," about Emily Previn, a 47-year old single woman. As the authors note:

> "In a short opening scene, Emily chokes on her food while eating dinner alone in front of the television. After a short struggle, Emily collapses and dies. In the following scene, Emily's body can be seen lying on the kitchen floor, covered with ants. Emily's landlord and her neighbour enter her house following the neighbour's complaint about the pungent smell emanating from Emily's house. The two walk into the kitchen, and find Emily's decaying body."

It wasn't enough that Emily ended up alone, in a degraded position, eaten by ants, and stinking up the place. Soon the Fisher family piled on. (The Fishers were the main characters of *Six Feet Under*; they ran a funeral parlor out of their own home.) Nate said, "I don't think this woman had anyone in her life." Another character, Federico, who helped the Fishers with body restoration, said that Emily's body was too far gone to be restored. Nate then became even crueler, speculating that perhaps Emily was "some vicious asshole, just twisted and evil." Ruth, the mother of Nate and David and Claire, was deeply disturbed by what happened to Emily.

What intrigued the sociologists about the story of Emily Previn is that eventually, a much more dignified interpretation was offered, both by Claire and by Ruth. Each in turn floated the idea that Emily may have been living a life that she chose and that she enjoyed.

Ruth grappled with her own preoccupation with Emily's story, until she figured out why, and gathered her family around her to explain: "I don't want to turn into her." Nate insists that she needn't worry because she has her three children. But Ruth isn't buying it:

> "I do not. Nate, you've been walking around like a zombie for months. David, you've been lying in bed in the middle of the day, God knows

why...Claire, I can't even look in your direction without having you act like it's an incredible imposition. All I want is for us not to act like strangers. I want intimacy."

Ruth was the only one to articulate her craving for the intimacy that was missing from her life. All the Fishers, though, were struggling "with their predicaments and heartaches alone." Nate, for example, had a disease that could prove fatal, but he was keeping that terrifying possibility to himself.

So there it is – a very different explanation for why some people are drawn to stories about the person who dies alone. It is an explanation that urges us to look past our usual understandings and presumptions. Just because a person is surrounded by family does not mean that they are protected from profound loneliness. Maybe that's one of the scariest possibilities: that you did everything "right" – you got married, you had kids...you even live with your kids. And yet, you too could die "alone" in the most painful sense of the word. You *feel* truly alone, even though you have family all around you.

**Reference**: Yodovich, N., & Lahad, K. (2017). 'I don't think this woman had anyone in her life': Loneliness and singlehood in *Six Feet Under*. *European Journal of Women's Studies*.

# The Stunning Appeal of a Story about a Man Who Died Alone

When the *New York Times* published "The Lonely Death of George Bell," readers could not get enough of it. Within a day, it had racked up more than 1,300 comments. For several days, it sat atop the lists of the "Most Viewed" and "Most Emailed" articles. Printed, the article goes on for 27 pages. Probably what was most important in drawing people in, though, was what came first: the "lonely death" highlighted in the title, the horrible huge picture of a totally trashed room at the top of the article, and the opening lines:

> "They found him in a living room, crumpled up, on the mottled carpet. The police did. Sniffing a fetid odor, a neighbor had called 911."

This is not some random human-interest story. This is a morality tale, a scare story aimed directly at anyone who would dare to live single and live alone.

The story is illustrated by 16 photos. Of the first seven, four of them are pictures of filth. It is hard to escape the implication that George Bell's life was garbage.

The reporter takes us through pages and pages of descriptions of New York City officials' often futile attempts to find George Bell's family or friends. That implication is clear, too – he doesn't have any.

Got it, single people? Stay single, live in a place of your own, and your life, too, will match the trash in George Bell's place. You, too, will die without a soul who cares about you. You'll end up "crumpled on a mottled carpet," left undiscovered until someone notices "a fetid odor."

Readers who persist past the grim beginnings, and the ominous middle, will find that George Bell's life was not exactly the horror story they were led to believe. He did have friends and family in his life. He and three close friends had worked as movers for years. He also stayed in touch with Eleanore, a woman he had always loved. On the Valentine's Day before he died, she sent him a card with the note, "George, think of you often with love."

Eleanore married someone else, but she did not remarry after her husband died in 2002. She lived alone.

Wrong move, Eleanore! The *Times* lets us know that she got what was coming to her – a fate like George's:

> "Her life finished up a lot like his. She lived alone, in a trailer. She died of a heart attack. A neighbor who cleared her snow found her. She had gotten obese. Her brother had her creamated."

Keep reading to the very end of the article and you will discover that George Bell did have a good friend (Frank) even at the end of his life. In fact, for the 15 years they had known each other, right up to the week before George died, George and Frank met regularly at a local bar. They got together every Saturday. They went fishing, shopping, and just passed the time in each other's company. They were together buying the shrimp that was on sale at the shopping center, probably just days before George died.

The bartender, who saw George and Frank together all the time, was apparently not moved by their friendship. Instead, he said, "George was in a lot of pain. I think he was just waiting to die, had lived enough." (He was 72.)

In case we single people missed the lesson, the reporter rammed it home in a stand-alone, single-sentence paragraph:

> "It was as if sadness had killed George Bell."

In addition to the 15-year friendship that lasted until the day he died, George Bell also had something else – money. His bank accounts had $215,000. His apartment sold for $225,000 and his car for $9,500. If he wanted to live some other way, he could have afforded that.

Toward the beginning of the article, we are told that of the 50,000 people who die each year in New York, for a small number of them:

> "No one mourns the conclusion of a life. They are just a name added to the death tables. In the year 2014, George Bell, age 72, was among those names."

So, George's friend of 15 years doesn't count as someone who mourned the end of his life?

Remember, George had just spent time with Frank right before he died. They had gotten together, as they always had, since 2004. So George's demise got called a "lonely death" in the heading because no one was there the moment he drew his last breath?

Let me tell you about my father's death. He died on the cold, hard floor of the bathroom of a hospital room, after midnight, having collapsed from an abdominal aneurysm. I don't know how long he lay there, helpless and all alone, until a nurse discovered him.

But he had a wife and four of us "kids" who would have done anything for him. No one would ever write a headline about his "lonely death." But in those final moments, was he really any less alone or lonely than George Bell? Or maybe we're just not allowed to think that way about people who are married – especially if they are married with children. Those people did everything right. There are no lessons to be learned. They did not live single and they did not live alone. Nothing to see here.

The *Times* reporter put a tremendous amount of time into the reporting and writing of the story about Poor George. The paper could have saved its resources and simply asked to reprint the relevant section of Eric Klinenberg's book, *Going Solo*. He reported, in detail, on what happened after Mary Ann died alone, in much the same way that the *Times* did with George Bell. At the very end of the section on Mary Ann, Klinenberg describes conversations with two of her neighbors. One said she had no visitors, ever, and seemed sad and lonely. The other said, "She was a nice person. All the time she talked to us. She talked with my son."

Here's how Klinenberg ended his story of Mary Ann. I think it is the proper moral of Mary Ann's story and George's:

> "Talking with [the two neighbors] helps me understand something about what happens when truly isolated people die alone. In most cases, we can't actually know whether their solitude was a source of sadness, or satisfaction. Whether they lived and died without friends or family nearby because they preferred it that way, or because something went wrong once and they couldn't get it right. When we hear about someone like Mary Ann, we can't help but project some of our own feelings into her story. And our reactions may say as much about each of us as they do about the deceased."

# 58

# Brilliant Author and Hospice Worker Makes the Case that Some People Want to Die Alone

Some stories are lodged so deeply in our cultural consciousness that we never challenge them. They are told in the same way, over and over again.

One of those stories is about dying alone. When you start reading such a story, or watching it on TV or in the movies, you know what you are in for. It is going to be a sad, sad story about a sad person living a sad life. You know the lesson you are supposed to learn: don't live like that person. Live a different way, so you won't die alone.

Ann Neumann, author of _The Good Death_, begs to disagree. In a brilliant article published in *The Baffler*, Neumann argues that dying alone is not a character flaw. It is not a personal failure. Dying alone – and living alone – are instead "deeply rooted in our social institutions." What more, it is presumptuous to believe that everyone who dies alone wants to be saved from that way of exiting the world; some, in fact, prefer it.

Neumann was intrigued (as was I) with the wildly popular 2015 story in the *New York Times*, "The lonely death of George Bell." In the cultural narrative about dying alone, the body of the person who dies alone will remain undiscovered until someone notices the smell. That happened to George Bell. Bell also had a problem with hoarding and the *Times* underscored that with graphic photos.

In my critique of the *Times* article, I pointed out that Bell was not the isolated and lonely man that the "lonely death" title insisted he was. He had friends throughout his life, including a close friend he saw regularly right up until the time he died. Among the belongings found in his apartment was a card from the most recent Valentine's Day from a woman he loved. It said, "George, think of you often with love."

Neumann was interested in something else about George Bell: He had more than $200,000 in his bank account. Too many other seniors are poor when they die. Although Bell's financial resources did not save him from the kind of death that scares people, money is often a powerful determinant of what our final days look like. That's not what the *Times* story was about, but it should have been.

By focusing on personal stories of how people live their lives and how they should better themselves, our cultural narratives distract us from far more significant considerations. As Neumann explains, those considerations include "systemic issues like poverty, racial and gender disparity, lack of caregiver resources, and a health care system that saves its best for those who can pay top dollar." Even hospice care, initially envisioned as a way that *all* dying patients could die in comfort away from instrument-filled hospital rooms, "has stubbornly remained a white people service."

Woven throughout Ann Neumann's article was the story of the growing popularity of "death doulas," who are trained to help those who are dying. Quoting Lizzy Miles, Neumann notes that hospices "have entire programs devoted to assuring patients and families that they will not ever be alone. Some of them are actually called, 'No one dies alone' or NODA.'"

Neumann was trained in hospice care in 2008. She has spent years studying and writing about death and dying. Instead of peddling NODA, she has a different idea:

> "Maybe, just maybe, dying patients really don't mind slipping out the door by themselves, kissing sweet earth goodbye without getting kisses back, riding off into the sunset without a sidekick."

**VIII**

# Keep on Reading:
# Insights from Great Books on Solitude

# Insights from the Most Renowned Book on Solitude

In a culture obsessed with marriage and coupling, solitude gets short shrift. There is, though, one esteemed book on the topic that has maintained its lofty status more than a quarter-century after its initial publication in 1988. I'm talking about the psychiatrist Anthony Storr's "*Solitude: A Return to Self.*"

The back cover of a recent printing of the book poses this question: "In the supreme importance that we place on intimate relationships, have we overlooked the deep, sustaining power of solitude in human life?" Of course, Anthony Storr's answer is yes.

Here are just a few key quotes and insights from *Solitude*.

> "...some development of the capacity to be alone is necessary if the brain is to function at its best, and if the individual is to fulfill his highest potential. Human beings easily become alienated from their own deepest needs and feelings. Learning, thinking, innovation, and maintaining contact with one's own inner world are all facilitated by solitude."

> "The capacity to form attachments...is considered evidence of emotional maturity...Whether there may be other criteria of emotional maturity, like the capacity to be alone, is seldom taken into account."

> Attachment theory "does less than justice to the importance of work, to the emotional significance of what goes on in the mind of the individual when he is alone, and, more especially, to the central place occupied by the imagination in those who are capable of creative achievement. Intimate attachments are *a* hub around which a person's life revolves, not necessarily *the* hub."

"The capacity to be alone is a valuable resource when changes of mental attitude are required. After major alterations in circumstances, fundamental reappraisal of the significance and meaning of existence may be needed. In a culture in which interpersonal relationships are generally considered to be the answer to every form of distress, it is sometimes difficult to persuade well-meaning helpers that solitude can be as therapeutic as emotional support."

"The modern assumption that intimate relationships are essential to personal fulfillment tends to make us neglect the significance of relationships which are not so intimate."

"In the present climate, there is a danger that love is being idealized as the only path to salvation. When Freud was asked what constituted psychological health, he gave as his answer the ability to love and work. We have over-emphasized the former, and paid too little attention to the latter."

"...there is always an element of uncertainty in interpersonal relationships which should preclude them from being idealized as an absolute or seen as constituting the only path toward personal fulfillment. It may be our idealization of interpersonal relationships in the West that causes marriage, supposedly the most intimate tie, to be so unstable. If we did not look to marriage as the principal source of happiness, fewer marriages would end in tears."

"Contemporary Western culture makes the peace of solitude difficult to attain...Indeed, noise is so ubiquitous that many people evidently feel uncomfortable in its absence."

"Even those who have the happiest relationships with others need something other than those relationships to complete their fulfillment."

"Everyone needs interests as well as interpersonal relationships; and interests, as well as relationships, play an important part in defining individual identity and in giving meaning to a person's life."

"The *need* to be alone differs from the *capacity* to be alone in its suggestion that, at times, other people constitute a hindrance, interference, or threat."

"...some of the most profound and healing psychological experiences which individuals encounter take place internally, and are only distantly related, if at all, to interaction with other human beings."

# How to be Alone: 14 Quips and Tips

Behold, Sara Maitland's book, _How to Be Alone_. I know what you badasses are thinking – you already know how to be alone. So true. Still, there is much to savor in the book.

Here are 14 of my favorite quips and quotes from _How to Be Alone_:

1. "Being single, being alone – together with smoking – is one of the few things that complete strangers feel free to comment on rudely: it is so dreadful a state (and probably, like smoking, your own fault) that the normal social requirements of manners and tolerance are superseded."

2. "...asking people why they like being alone or what they get out of it (and of course listening to their answers) is one very effective way of learning about being alone and enjoying it."

3. "It is not odd to live alone."

4. "...very often when people say something is 'unnatural', they really mean 'I do not approve of it'."

5. "...the biggest danger of solitude is fear – and often fear mixed with both the derision and judgment of others...Fear is more likely to undermine health than being alone is."

6. On why single people sometimes stereotype other single people, and themselves: "...if you tell people enough times that they are unhappy, incomplete, possibly insane and definitely selfish there is bound to come a grey morning when they wake up with the beginning of a nasty cold and wonder if they are lonely rather than simply 'alone.'

7. About "the two most common tactics for evading the terror of solitude": (1) "...denigrating those who do not fear it, especially if they claim to enjoy it, and stereotyping them as 'miserable', 'selfish', 'crazy', or 'perverse' (sad, mad, and bad)." (2) "...infinitely extending our social

contacts as a sort of insurance policy, which social media makes increasingly possible." [Maitland believes that both are "singularly ineffective."]

8. "The best treatment for a non-clinical fear of being alone is learning more about it and exposing yourself to solitude, initially in very low 'doses'."

9. "The joy of long periods of solitude has also increased my joy in non-solitude: I love my children, my friends, my colleagues as much as ever, and I attend to them better when I am with them – and enjoy them more. But, above all, I like me better. I think there is more of me to like – a deep spaciousness of self, joyful, creatively and professionally productive and alert to both my interior and exterior life."

10. "It feels strange to me that people who choose to be alone in the comfort of their own house are regarded, and too often treated, as weirdos, while those who to choose be alone several thousand feet above the snowline or in a tiny boat in the middle of the Pacific Ocean are perceived as heroes."

11. Solo adventurers "are doing these things to explore their own inner worlds as much as the external one."

12. On why solitude is good for creativity: "...because creating something yourself, of your own, uniquely, requires a kind of personal freedom, a lack of inhibition, a capacity not to glance over your shoulder at the opinions of others."

13. Talking to grown-ups about children: "Neither you nor they can know which sort of person they are if they cannot ever try out solitude."

14. "Most of us have a dream of doing something in particular which we have never been able to find anyone to do with us. And the answer is simple, really: do it with yourself."

## "Liberty Is a Better Husband"

A wonderfully quotable and insightful book for people who love their solitude is Kate Bolick's _Spinster: Making a Life of One's Own_. Here, I'll share some of my favorite observations from the book. And because _Spinster_ does not include among the five inspirational figures from the past anyone who stayed single for life, I will also add a few words of wisdom from someone who did, Louisa May Alcott.

About her own experiences, Kate Bolick offers these thoughts:

- From her Dec 23, 1997 journal entry: "What a luxury, to be twenty-five and unattached..."

- A few years later: "What bothered me was the assumption that because I was a woman in her early thirties, I must be 'desperate' for marriage."

- Later still: "I was most alive when alone, negotiating odd encounters on the subway, surging along the sidewalk with a million faceless others. It was an expansive sensation, evasive, addictive."

- After a long-term relationship ended: "For the first time, I felt like an actual person who lives in the world and could carry on a conversation with another adult about something other than the minutiae of what I did that day and whose turn it was to get the groceries. Coupling, I realized, can encourage a fairly static way of being...Along with meeting new people I was discovering a new self."

Some cultural and historical observations:

- "It's amazing, really, how deftly we hold in our collective consciousness this disconnect between what we want marriage to be and how so many marriages actually turn out."

- Despite all the blogs that were online by 2003, there were still no "serious conversations about the lives of unmarried women. Instead, whatever candor had erupted in the 1960s had been sucked into a black hole of constant chatter about dating, sex, marriage, children. The notion of not marrying was apparently so outlandish that it was consigned to fiction, whether chick-lit or television, as if the thought of single women was so threatening we had no choice but to trivialize it."

- About Edna St. Vincent Millay living "fully and without deference to convention. This embrace of possibility, and willingness to improvise rather than 'nail down' a life discomfits and disrupts now as much as it did then."

- "The flapper vanished with the Great Depression, as did anything smacking of frivolity and hedonism, at which point, for the first time in forty years, the single woman's status dropped. Now that heterosexual sex was considered integral to mental health, unmarried women were increasingly represented as lonely, celibate spinsters. Meanwhile, the labor market became a battlefield. With so many people out of work, jobs became the privilege of men with families to feed – as if many single women weren't also supporting their parents, siblings, and families."

- Why "the crazy bag lady" is the scariest: "...she's living proof of what it means to not be loved. Her apparition will endure as long as women consider the love of a man the most supreme of all social validations."

Some insights from other people mentioned in *Spinster*:

- From Vivian Gornick, about waking up the morning after leaving her husband: "The *idea* of love seemed an invasion. I had thoughts to think, a craft to learn, a self to discover. Solitude was a gift. A world was waiting to welcome me if I was willing to enter it alone."

- From Neith Boyce (who wrote the "Bachelor Girl" column for *Vogue* magazine – starting in 1898!), on seeing the bright smile of her cousin on her wedding day: "Surely marriage was nothing to look so exuberant about, and coming down the aisle chatting and smiling to one another, as though they were dinner partners, seemed all wrong. Considering what marriage led to – children, bills, quarrels, the frightening forced association of two human beings – surely it was nothing to be light-minded about. [She] thought there should be a touch of sackcloth and ashes about it."

And now for some wisdom from Louisa May Alcott, as noted by Jean R. Freedman in her *Washington Post* article:

- "I'd rather be a free spinster and paddle my own canoe."

- "...liberty is a better husband than love to many of us."

- "My sisters, don't be afraid of the words, 'old maid,' for it is in your power to make this a term of honor, not reproach."

# 62

# Why True Loners Are Awesome – And Why So Many People Thought They Weren't

Loners get a bad rap. They are smeared as criminals, crazy people, haters, and people no one would ever want to befriend. All that is wrong.

If you want to understand why, there is no better source than the book by Anneli Rufus, Party of One: The Loners' Manifesto. Loners, Rufus explains, are people who prefer to be alone. Not all the time, but a lot of the time. The *preference* for being alone is what distinguishes true loners from pseudo-loners, those people who may look like loners but really aren't.

There are lots of reasons why people might spend a lot of time alone even though they don't want to. Maybe they are outcasts, who would love to be included but have instead been rejected. Maybe they have serious problems. Maybe they have something to hide. Those people are not true loners.

*Party of One* is a brilliant exploration of loners in relation to popular culture, advertising, technology, art, literature, religion, community, friendship, love, sex, and eccentricity. It is about the places loners love to go and to live. It is about their clothes, their childhoods, and their sanity.

It is not a new book, but it is a book I keep coming back to. Here I want to share with you some quotes from Anneli Rufus on key themes.

**The true meaning of 'loner'**

A loner is "someone who prefers to be alone."

With a nod to *Twelfth Night*, Rufus notes that loners "are at our best when least in company."

"We do not require company. The opposite: in varying degrees, it bores us, drains us, makes our eyes glaze over."

"We need our space."

185

"Loner" is not a synonym for 'misanthrope." Nor is it one for 'hermit,' 'celibate,' or 'outcast.' It is just that we are very selective. *Verrry* selective."

## The special strengths of loners

"We are the ones who know how to entertain ourselves. How to learn without taking a class. How to contemplate and how to create."

Loners "have an innate advantage when it comes to being brave [and] when faced with the unknown. An advantage when it comes to being mindful...Innate advantages when it comes to imagination, concentration, inner discipline...A talent for seldom being bored."

## What 'alone' means to a loner

"The word *alone* should not, for us, ring cold and hollow, but hot. Pulsing with potentiality. Alone as in distinct. Alone as in, Alone in his field. As in, Stand alone. As in, like it or not, Leave me alone."

"...for loners, the idea of solitude is not some stark departure from our normal state. *We* do not need writers to tell us how lovely apartness is, how sacred it was to the sages, what it did for Thoreau, that we must demand it."

## Loners and their friends

"Of course loners have friends. Fewer than most nonloners have, maybe. But loners, with our extra capacity for concentration, focus, our fewer distractions, make excellent friends."

"For some loners, a paucity of friends is a matter of time. There is simply too much to do alone, no time to spare...And time shared, even with true friends, often requires loners to put in *extra* time alone, overtime, to recharge."

As for nonloners: "Sometimes it seems they would rather have *anyone* around than no one."

## Loners as romantic partners

"Loners have nothing against love, but are more careful about it."

"Loners, if you can catch them, are well worth the trouble." They are "curious, vigilant, full of surprises. They do not cling."

## Loners and shyness

"...there is significant overlap between shy people and loners." But "not all shy people are loners nor are all loners shy."

## Loners, mental health, and mental health professionals

"I am not crazy now, but forced to act like a nonloner for an extended period, I might *go* crazy."

About mental health professionals: "If they ask whether we are alone by choice, they are doing their job. If they do not try to dissuade us, fine. If they move on from there to praise our self-awareness, our skill at choosing and living as we choose, they are doing their job. If they show us how to handle the slander, ensure, jokes, and misapprehension...then they are doing their job."

## Loners and criminals – don't confuse the two

"*He was a loner* is a crime-story cliché...But learning the true stories of criminals who are called loners in the press reveals, with striking frequency, that these are not genuine loners...*They do not wish to be alone. Their dislike of being alone is what drives them to violence.*"

"...it takes a *social* man to become so possessive, so enmeshed with others, that his rage and jealousy over a breakup make him want to kill."

## Loner children

"Some kids...*like* to play alone. Others...are outcasts."

## Loners and the purported death of civilization

"...we no longer all need to be social animals in order to survive as a species. Mandatory social interaction is an evolutionary remnant which those who wish to may discard."

# About the Author

Bella DePaulo (Ph.D., Harvard University) writes myth-busting, consciousness-raising, totally unapologetic books on single life. The *Atlantic* magazine has described her as "America's foremost thinker and writer on the single experience." She is the award-winning author of *Singled Out: How Singles Are Stereotyped, Stigmatized, and Ignored, and Still Live Happily Ever After*, and has been writing the "Living Single" blog for *Psychology Today* since 2008.

Dr. DePaulo's writings have been published in the *New York Times*, the *Washington Post*, *Time* magazine, and many other places. Her TEDx talk, "What no one ever told you about people who are single," was an instant hit. "Alone: The Badass Psychology of People Who Like Being Alone" is her 20th book.

After two decades as a Professor of Psychology at the University of Virginia, Dr. DePaulo moved to the west coast in the year 2000 for what was supposed to be a 1-year sabbatical at the University of California at Santa Barbara. She never returned. She is currently an Academic Affiliate in Psychological and Brain Sciences at UCSB. Visit Bella DePaulo's website at BellaDePaulo.com.

Made in the USA
Las Vegas, NV
07 September 2024

94933531R00111